Final Scrum

For my brother, Ashley, who has overcome so much and turned out to be the extraordinary man he is. With my love.

Final Scrum

Rugby Internationals Killed in the Second World War

Nigel McCrery

Pen & Sword
MILITARY

First published in Great Britain in 2018 by
Pen & Sword Military
An imprint of
Pen & Sword Books Ltd
47 Church Street
Barnsley
South Yorkshire
S70 2AS

Copyright © Nigel McCrery 2018

ISBN 978 1 47389 450 1

The right of Nigel McCrery to be identified as Author of this work has been asserted
by him in accordance with the Copyright, Designs and Patents Act 1988.

A CIP catalogue entry for this book is available from the British Library.

Typeset in 10pt Dante by
Mac Style

Printed and bound in the UK by TJ International Ltd, Padstow, Cornwall

Pen & Sword Books Limited incorporates the imprints of Atlas,
Archaeology, Aviation, Discovery, Family History, Fiction, History,
Maritime, Military,
Military Classics, Politics, Select, Transport, True Crime, Air World,
Frontline Publishing, Leo Cooper, Remember When, Seaforth Publishing,
The Praetorian Press, Wharncliffe Local History, Wharncliffe Transport,
Wharncliffe True Crime and White Owl.

For a complete list of Pen & Sword titles please contact
PEN & SWORD BOOKS LIMITED
47 Church Street, Barnsley, South Yorkshire, S70 2AS, England
E-mail: enquiries@pen-and-sword.co.uk
Website: www.pen-and-sword.co.uk

Contents

Australia

England

France

Acknowledgments

Michael Rowe, rugby historian, for his exceptional work on the Scotland players. Alan Clay, for taking the time and trouble to help with the research whenever he could.

Thanks are due to Richard Steel whose knowledge of rugby history is utterly astounding, and who was typically generous with his time and expertise on the Scottish entries. I am equally grateful for the help provided by Phil McGowan, Debbie Mason and all the staff at the excellent new World Rugby Museum in Twickenham, as well as Dai Richards, also of the World Rugby Museum (on-line) for his help, advice and never-ending supply of information and sources. Many of the schools and colleges attended by these young men now have excellent on-line archives, and my thanks in particular to Sedbergh, Fettes and George Watson's for the information thus provided.

The personal touch remains the most important, and Fraser Simm at George Heriot's Trust, Fiona Hooper at George Watson's College, David Amdurer at Strathallan School, David McDowell and Craig Marshall at Fettes College, and Alastair Allanach at the Royal High School Club were all immensely helpful. Matt Jones, Pen & Sword a first rate man, who has held my hand through all the books I have written and without whose calm advice and kindness I'm not sure any would have been written. Henry Wilson at Pen & Sword for taking on the book. Barnaby Blacker my long-suffering editor, Jon Wilkinson, Katie Eaton, Mat Blurton and Katie Noble all at Pen & Sword. Medals Forum (on- line), the Second World War Forum (on-line), Great War Forum (on-line). The late and much missed inspiration, one of the best men I ever knew, Hal Giblin for his encouragement. Brian Turner, medal collector and researcher for his endless help. Cambridge University, Oxford University. I hope there isn't anyone I have missed, if I have my apologies and I will be sure to include you in future editions.

A few notes on the Scottish section. Many memorials and lists include A.W. Symington among the Second World War dead. However, research undertaken by David McDowell at Fettes College shows that Symington, an international with a distinguished service record in the First World War, was a civilian when he died of a heart attack in 1941.

Additionally, W.A. Ross is often shown as having been killed in September 1942. In fact, his death occurred a year earlier, as shown on the excellent website of the Scottish Military Research Group Commemoration Project.

Nigel McCrery, February 2018

Introduction

My passion, inherited from my father, is the First World War, and having now written several books on sporting greats who died during that awful war I was surprised when Pen & Sword asked me if I would be interested in writing a few books on Second World War sporting icons who lost their lives during that equally dreadful conflict. I wasn't sure at first but now I'm glad I did. I've started the series with *The Coming Storm*, about the test and first-class cricketers who died during the Second World War. So fascinated did I become by their stories and ultimate sacrifice that writing these books became more of a passion than a duty. This second book, *Final Scrum*, is about international rugby players, and as with *The Coming Storm* I have found researching the Second World War much harder than the First. France in particular was difficult with very little information available (also they were kicked out of the Nations for professionalism in 1931 which didn't help), and none when it comes to Germany and Rumania, something I hope to remedy in following editions. In view of this I have concentrated on England, Scotland, Wales, Ireland, France, Australia and New Zealand. In total I have discovered fifty-seven players who died or lost their lives as a result of the conflict. I would also like to take this opportunity to thank my co-author, Michael Rowe, for his first-class work on the Scottish internationals, an extremely important part of the book and a job very well done.

If any mistakes have been made in the writing of this book please feel free to point them out, and as long as you're not rude and I'm sure you wouldn't be I'll be happy to include them in the next edition. Also if you feel anyone has been missed, once again please contact me, and if correct I will include in the next edition. Although I have done my best to include a photograph of every international, there are a few missing. If anyone can help with this it would be much appreciated. I would also like to point out that all the money made from this book will go to the charity 'Care After Combat', a charity that cares for service personnel who have had problems for a variety of reasons since leaving the forces – a very worthwhile cause. I hope you enjoy and learn from this book. Buying it or reading a copy helps to keep the memory of these most exceptional men and their sacrifice remembered forever.

Rugby Union in the Second World War

If enthusiasm and patriotic excitement had marked rugby's reaction to the outbreak of the First World War there would be no repeat in September 1939. The game, like the rest of society, met the declaration of war with a grim recognition of the struggle and sacrifice to come.

Memories of the Great War still, of course, dominated national life. For the most part, the young men commemorated in this book were already born when that conflict had ended only 21 years before. Rugby's innumerable committees and corridors of power were filled with men who had experienced the terrors of war first-hand. The indefatigability of some, like Scotland's Pat Munro and England's Norman Wodehouse, would mean that they served in both wars before paying the ultimate sacrifice.

There was a quick and universal recognition that the outbreak of war meant an end to normal rugby life. Unlike 1914, when there was a certain amount of muddle and contradiction in the sport's reaction, the season was suspended almost immediately. International competition, overseas tours and club games all ceased to exist in the normal fashion for the duration of the war.

Which is not to say that there was no rugby during the war – far from it. Rugby, like sport generally, was recognised as an ideal way of occupying young men thrown together in large numbers. The military authorities recognised, as they always had, that sport helped develop leadership, physical fitness and *esprit de corps*. The civilian powers saw in rugby an ideal way of providing cheap entertainment to a hard-pressed population, and the attendances at club and service matches during the conflict justified their faith.

The structure of the sport during the war varied but became, as one might expect, generally more organised and structured towards the end of the conflict. Some clubs closed for the duration, while others continued to operate. In Britain the services teams came to a much greater prominence than had previously been the case, regularly turning out sides packed with pre-war internationals.

In a repeat of the decision taken during the First World War, the authorities lifted the ban on rugby league players competing in the union code. The sport seemed to revel in the new found freedom, organising matches (under union rules) between players of the different codes within individual units, culminating in a victory for the Combined Services rugby league team over their union counterparts. More routinely, league players (many of them ex-union stars) enjoyed testing themselves in a sport from which they were ordinarily outlawed.

In 1939 the British unions had decided to overturn the suspension of France from the Five Nations tournament, having apparently overcome their doubts as to the amateur status of the Gallic game. If war meant that the formal French return would be delayed until 1947, the 'phoney war' saw plenty of rugby opportunities for the allied troops in France, culminating in a match between the British Army and France in February 1940.

Germany does not feature highly in rugby's history. However the country was a force in the sport during the inter-war years when France, banned from competing against the British sides, was looking for alternative competition.

Reputedly Hitler, seeing rugby as too 'English', was one of the factors behind the decline of the game in his country. Führer disapproval notwithstanding, German, Italian and Romanian sides were playing capped internationals just days before the dictator conclusively ended the phoney war in May 1940. Sixteen German internationals would be killed in the war.

France's military capitulation marks the darkest day in the nation's history and the behaviour of the French Federation during the occupation is equally dismal. Seen as close – and in many cases enthusiastic – collaborators with the Vichy regime, the union authorities took the opportunity to effectively eliminate rugby league in the country, confiscating the assets of league clubs and forcing players to join the union code.

More positively, pre-war international Jacques Chaban-Delmas served with distinction in the resistance and would go on to serve as mayor of Bordeaux and eventually prime minister under President Pompidou. A total of eight French internationals would be killed in the war.

Later in the war a series of services international matches were played. With so many of the sport's best players serving overseas or otherwise unavailable, these could never match the standard of true internationals. They were successful in generating interest and excitement however, as well as providing opportunities for genuinely first-class rugby for many young players who were otherwise deprived of the opportunity.

As in the First World War, the allies celebrated victory with an international rugby competition. In 1919 there was the King's Cup, regarded by many as a prototype Rugby World Cup and – like the first edition of the genuine RWC – won by New Zealand. The 1946 equivalent was less closely organised and consisted of a series of matches over a number of months, known as the *Victory Internationals*. This time there was no outright victor, and while France and the home nations had individual teams, the Kiwis, Australians, South Africans and others had to be content with composite 'British Empire' sides.

There was, however, no getting away from New Zealand rugby might. Playing under the relatively innocuous name of 'Second New Zealand Expeditionary Force Rugby Team' the *Kiwis* gave a more than passable imitation of the All Blacks and drew huge crowds wherever they went. In a sign that things really were getting back to normal, the New Zealanders played 33 matches, won 29 and ended with an aggregate score of 605-185.

The 1946/47 season saw rugby approach its pre-war normality. Many players from of the *Kiwis* team arrived home in New Zealand just in time to transform into genuine All Blacks and comfortably win a short series against Australia. France marked their delayed return to the Five Nations with a New Year's Day victory over Scotland, eventually finishing a creditable fourth behind the winners Wales.

Michael Rowe, December 2017

Australia

VX603 Lance Bombardier Frederick Raymond Kerr
Australia
2/2nd Field Regiment, Royal Australian Army
One test
Died 23 April 1941, aged 22
Number 8

'The All Blacks considered Kerr the best forward they met on their tour.'

Frederick Raymond Kerr was born on 25 April 1918 in St Kilda, Victoria, Australia. He was the son of William Frederick and Edith Dorothy Kerr, of Middle Park. He was educated at Melbourne High School.

Kerr began his sporting life playing Australian Rules football for the Power House Club but was soon attracted to rugby union and began playing for Victoria Rugby Club as a flanker. He must have impressed because he was chosen to play for Australia against New Zealand on 23 July 1938 at the Sydney cricket ground. Australia went down 9-24, Max Carpenter kicking three penalties. Kerr was one of five players who made their debut for Australia that day. Although Kerr played well, he was dropped and never again represented his country. Many thought Kerr was unfairly dropped – a brutal reaction by the

Memorial window at Melbourne High School, Australia.

selectors to the loss of the first test. One journalist later commented, 'The All Blacks considered Kerr the best forward they met on their tour.'

On the outbreak of war Kerr enlisted into the ranks of the Australian Army Field Artillery, being promoted to lance bombardier with the 2/2 Field Regiment (raised on 13 October 1939 in Victoria). The regiment was assigned to the 6th Division and was posted to North Africa in 1940, later being sent to Greece. Frederick Kerr was killed on 23 April 1941, almost certainly during the battle for the Thermopylae position.

Realizing that the Allied forces were evacuating their troops by ship from Volos and Piraeus, the Germans laid plans to try to stop the evacuation and mop up any remaining allied resistance. To this end they committed the 2nd and 5th Panzer Divisions, the 1st SS Motorised Infantry Regiment and both mountain divisions in pursuit of the Allied forces. To give the army time to get away a rearguard action was organized at the historic Thermopylae pass, seen as the gateway to Athens. The pass was made famous for the last stand of the Spartan army who defended the pass against 150,000 Persians in 480 BC. 'Go tell the Spartans, thou who passest by, that here, obedient to their laws, we lie.'

General Freyberg's 2nd New Zealand Division was given the task of defending the coastal pass while Mackay's 6th Australian Division was to hold the village of Brallos. After a historic defence, orders were received to evacuate on 23 April. However they did leave the two positions with a brigade each. These brigades, the 19th Australian and 6th New Zealand were to hold the passes for as long as possible, allowing the other units to withdraw. It was during this retreat that the brave Frederick Kerr was killed.

The following day, the 24th, at 11.30am, the Germans launched an all-out attack. The allies held out for twenty-four hours and, having achieved their objective, pulled back towards the evacuation beaches, costing the Germans fifteen tanks and dozens of casualties in the process. After the battle General Mackay said, 'I did not dream of evacuation; I thought that we'd hang on for about a fortnight and be beaten by weight of numbers.'

Kerr's body was never recovered and he is commemorated on the Athens Memorial, face 10.

The Athens Memorial.

**Lieutenant Clifford Walter Patrick
(Haggis) Lang
Australia
Two tests
2/2 Pioneer Battalion
Died 4 March 1942, aged 32
Prop**

*A natural prop forward, he was both tough and hard. Standing 6ft 2in and
weighing 15 stone he was quick on his feet, powerful and could play in any
position asked of him*

Clifford Walter Patrick (Haggis) Lang was born on 2 July 1909 at Multan
in India. He was the son of Walter and Mary Agnes Anderson of Bletchley,
Buckinghamshire. He was educated at the Dollar Academy in Scotland where
he was in the first XV. On leaving school he played his club rugby for Bedford
RFC. A natural prop forward, he was tough and strong, and despite standing
6ft 2in and weighing 15 stone he was quick on his feet. He could play in any
position asked of him, although he did prefer the front row.

Eventually Lang decided to move to Australia and settled in Melbourne joining
the army and starting to play for Footscray RFC. Lang was part of the Footscray
team that won the Melbourne rugby premiership in both 1936 and 1937. Leaving
Footscray he joined Power House RFC also based in Melbourne. In the meantime
his career in the army was going well and he received a commission.

During the 1935 season Lang was selected to play for Victoria against the
New Zealand Maori. Unfortunately Victoria lost sixteen points to twenty-eight
in a hard-fought match. In 1937 he played for Victoria against the touring South
Africans (Springbok) team, Victoria going down once again, eleven points to
forty-five. Despite that Lang played well and came to notice. In 1938 the New
Zealand All Blacks toured Australia and Haggis Lang was selected to play in the
last two tests as a prop.

His first game came on 6 August 1938 at the Exhibition Ground, Brisbane.
Down 3-14 at half time, Australia fought hard during the second half. They pulled
back the score, but not enough and went down by fourteen points to twenty.
Lang's old friend Max Carpenter grounded two tries and Paul Collins one.
Carpenter also kicked a conversion and a penalty. Lang's next test appearance
came on 13 August at the Sydney cricket ground. Once again Australia went
down, this time by six points to fourteen, Mac Ramsay getting a try down and

Dooney Hayes kicking a penalty. It was Lang's last appearance in a test. He failed to be selected for the 1939 tour of Great Britain (the test that never happened).

During the war Lang served as a lieutenant with the 2/2 Pioneer Battalion, seeing action in Syria. On 19 February 1942, shortly after the fall of Singapore, Lieutenant Lang landed with his battalion in Java. Lieutenant Colonel Arthur Blackburn, who had been awarded the Victoria Cross in the First World War, was promoted to brigadier and given command of the 3,000 Australian troops on Java, the force being named 'Blackforce'. Between 28 February and 1 March 1942 the Japanese army began landing on Java, supported by the Imperial Japanese Army Air Force which bombed allied positions. Blackforce was quickly in action at Leuwiliang, losing over a hundred men killed, wounded and missing. The 2/2nd Pioneer Battalion fought hard killing around 300 of the enemy. The fighting continued until 8 March when the Dutch surrendered. Blackburn considered fighting on but the position was hopeless and he lacked supplies. He surrendered his forces on 12 March 1942. About 100 men from 'Blackforce' had been killed or wounded in battle and many of the 2,700 who became prisoners of war died in captivity. Unfortunately Lang was one of the one hundred killed, losing his life on 4 March 1942. Blackburn was distinctly unhappy about the surrender and wrote the following letter:

> ... *You are to take the first opportunity of telling your men that this surrender was not my choice or that of Gen. Sitwell. We were all placed under the command of the Commander in Chief NEI and he has ordered us to surrender. In view of medical reports on the dangers of living in the mountains and the impossibility of obtaining food in the mountains and the fact that no reasonable prospect of escape in ships from the South Coast exists, there was considered by Gen. Sitwell to be no alternative except to obey the order...*

Haggis Lang is commemorated in Jakarta War Cemetery, grave reference 6.C.5.

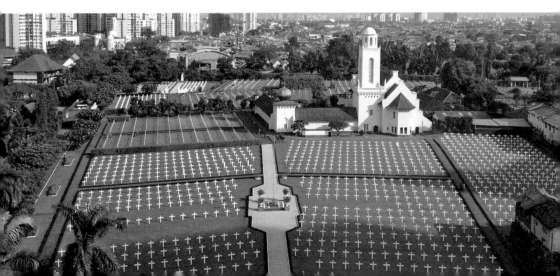

NX25468 Corporal Kenelm Mackenzie (Mac) Ramsay
Australia
Four tests
1 Independent Australian Infantry
Died 1 July 1942, aged 27
Position 8/lock/flanker

Twice as many Australians died in this one incident than were killed in the entire Vietnam War

Mac Ramsay was born on 27 August 1914 at Quirindi, New South Wales. He was the son of Kenelm Kierston and Jessie Gwendolene Ramsay of Bellevue Hill, New South Wales. He was educated at Tamworth High School and Hawkesbury Agricultural College, representing them both at rugby. He played his club rugby for Drummoyne (est 1873) in Sydney, representing them on thirteen occasions and Ranwick (est 1882) also based in Sydney, playing for them on sixty-six occasions. He scored fourteen tries for Ranwick and was an important part of their 1938 and 1940 grand final winning sides. He also represented New South Wales on thirteen occasions.

He so impressed the selectors that he was chosen to tour New Zealand with the Wallabies in 1936. Australia played in ten matches, losing eight and winning two. Ramsay played in the final test against the New Zealand Maori on 23 September 1936 at the FMG Stadium, Palmerston North. In a one-sided match Australia came out winners by six points to thirty-one. The Australians grounded six tries: Doug McLean got three down, Mac Ramsay scored on his debut, and Jack Kelaher and Vic Richards got one more each. Mike Gibbons and Russell Kelly kicked a conversion each while Ron Rankin kicked three. Rankin also kicked a penalty.

Ramsay went onto play in three more tests. He played against South Africa on 26 June 1937 at the Sydney cricket ground. South Africa took the match by five points to nine, Cyril Towers grounding a try and kicking the conversion. The following year, 1938, Ramsay was to represent Australia on two further occasions. Against New Zealand on 23 July at the Sydney cricket ground, New Zealand won the game easily by nine points to twenty-four. Australia failed to score a try but Max Carpenter kicked three penalties. A few weeks later on 13 August Ramsay represented Australia once again against New Zealand and again at the Sydney cricket ground. Going down by fourteen points to six Ramsay managed Australia's only try. Dooney Hayes kicked a penalty.

It was Ramsay's final test, although he was selected for the 'tour that never was' in 1939. Bill Hughes, the Australian prime minister, went to see the team, describing Ramsay as 'the perfect team man'. The tour was supposed to last ten months and take in twenty-eight matches and tests, however the day after the team set sail, Great Britain declared war on Nazi Germany and the tour was cancelled – but not before they had met the king and queen at Buckingham Palace and helped with Britain's home defences by filling sandbags.

Ramsay joined up, becoming a corporal in the Australian Army before joining the 1st Independent Company Commandos. His unit was posted to New Island, Papua New Guinea, in 1941. During the early part of 1942 the Japanese attacked the island in force. Ramsay's unit was ordered to retreat south relying on guerilla attacks to strike back as and when they could. Reaching the sea Ramsay boarded a small motorboat and almost got away, but the boat was spotted by the Japanese and bombed. Receiving several hits it sank quickly and Ramsay was forced to swim for it. He got to shore, but was captured and interned at Rabaul (the pre-war capital of Australian-mandated New Guinea) with hundreds of others. Eventually they were pushed aboard the 'Hell Ship' (so named because of the appalling conditions for the prisoners on these ships) the *Montevideo Maru* bound for Hainan Island as slave labour. Ramsay was among 845 Australian soldiers and 208 civilians on the converted merchant vessel. The ship wasn't to arrive at its destination.

The *Montevideo Maru*.

Final Scrum

On 22 June 1942, the *Montevideo Maru* embarked from Rabaul's port. It was unmarked and unescorted. On 30 June the ship was spotted by the US submarine *Sturgeon* close to the Philippines. Just before dawn on 1 July and unaware that it was a prison ship, the *Sturgeon* fired four torpedoes, hitting the ship along its length. The ship took eleven minutes to sink. Hundreds of men went into the water, clinging onto anything they could find to keep them afloat. They were scalded, burnt, choked by oil and flames, and drowned. It was later reported that as the survivors sank their comrades sang *Auld Lang Syne* as their exhausted friends slipped beneath the waves. A Japanese sailor later described the situation: 'People were jumping into the water. Thick oil was spreading across the sea. There were loud noises… metal wrenching, furniture crashing, people screaming… I was particularly impressed when they began to sing Auld Lang Syne as a tribute to their dead colleagues. Watching that I learned that Australians have big hearts.' On that day 1,054 prisoners drowned (178 non-commissioned officers, 667 soldiers, 209 civilians and sixty-eight Japanese guards). Twice as many Australians died in this one incident than were killed in the entire Vietnam War.

403320 Sergeant Michael Clifford
Australia
One test
Royal Australian Air Force, 452 Squadron
Died 9 October 1942, aged 26
Full Back

Member of the tragic 1939 test team

Michael Clifford was born on 28 April 1916 in Forbes, New South Wales. He was the son of Edward Timothy and Mary Assissium Clifford of Randwick. He was educated at St Stanislaus College, New South Wales, where he first played rugby, getting into the first XV. He played his club rugby for St George Rugby Club (the club's inaugural first grade appearance was on St George's Day, 23 April 1921, against Glebe at the Sydney Sports Ground). In 1937 Clifford made his state debut against Queensland, and played against both the Maroons and Victoria in each of the next two seasons.

He managed to get his place in the Australian line-up thanks to Ron Rankin getting injured and having to drop out. Clifford was then selected to take his place. Clifford played in only one test against the touring All Blacks, on 13 August 1938 at the Sydney cricket ground. New Zealand took the honours by fourteen points to six. Mac Ramsay got the ball down for the Australians and Dooney Hayes kicked a penalty. It was also noted that Clifford played well and did everything he could to hold the All Black attack in check.

Of the fifteen Australian players that turned out for this match six were to be later killed in the war: Mike Clifford, Dooney Hayes, Winston Ide, Frank Hutchinson, Haggis Lang and Kenelm Ramsay.

Clifford certainly impressed the selectors as he was chosen as a full back to go on the Australian 1939-40 tour of Great Britain. However the team had no sooner reached England than the Second World War broke out and, after taking part in some PR exercises including filling sandbags and meeting the king and queen, the team returned home. It became known as 'the tour that never was'. The return trip was considerably slower due to the ship having to keep zigzagging to avoid enemy torpedoes. When the ship docked at Bombay they managed to get a game in against the Gymkhana XV. All the new players were given a run in this match so they could claim the distinction of being internationals just in case they never got another chance. Australia won the match 21-0.

On his return to Australia, Clifford continued to play for St George whenever he could during the 1940 season. He joined the Royal Australian Air Force on 6 January 1941 and became attached to 452 Squadron. Taking off from Richmond at 09.15 on 9 October 1942 on a training run in Spitfire A58-25, F.VC BR471 (one of the first six to arrive in Australia), Clifford was doing an oxygen climb to 35,000 feet and he must have lost consciousness. His aircraft was seen to dive into the sea near Wamberal, Broken Bay, at 1011 hours, approximately a mile off shore. Clifford's body was found the following day off Shelly Beach. His funeral took place at St Anthony's Church, Clovelly, at 1030 hours on 12 October. He was later buried in the Roman Catholic section of Botany Cemetery, grave reference section 3, grave 71.

The Botany Cemetery.

Flying Officer Edwin Sautelle (Dooney) Hayes
Australian
Five tests
Royal Australian Air Force
Died 12 January 1943, aged 31
Centre

A member of the Caterpillar Club

Dooney Hayes was born on 10 August 1911 at Toowoomba, Queensland. He was the son of William George and Jane Caroline Hayes. He was educated at the Toowoomba Grammar School where he excelled at cricket and football and first learned to throw and run with a rugby ball. He played his club rugby for Past Grammars Rugby Club in Toowoomba.

Developing rapidly Hayes made his debut for Queensland in 1931 against New South Wales in the second match in Brisbane on 6 June 1931. He toured with Queensland and played in both interstate games in Sydney and dropped a field goal in the first match, which Queensland won 28-8. In 1932 Hayes played for Toowoomba against the All Blacks. He had an outstanding game, breaking down the All Blacks line and scoring a spectacular try early in the first half.

Dooney can be seen here, fifth from the right, as part of the Australia team that played New Zealand in 1934.

Having tried out unsuccessfully several times in 1933 Dooney moved to the GPS Club in Brisbane to try to improve his game as an inside centre. It clearly worked as he was named captain of the Queensland team that visited Sydney in June for the interstate matches.

When the New Zealand All Blacks arrived in Australia to defend the Bledisloe Cup, Dooney was selected to play in the first test. The match was played at the Sydney cricket ground on 11 August 1934. In front of a crowd of 40,000 Australia took the match by twenty-five points to eleven. Owen Bridle and Doug McLean got a try each and Cyril Towers grounded two. Alex Ross (captain) kicked two conversions and two penalties.

Selected for the second test on the 25 August, he played again at the Sydney cricket ground. In a hard-fought match they came out with honours, even at three points each. Had it not been for Dooney and sterling defense by the Australian back line the outcome might well have been different. Bob Loudon got the ball down for Australia.

With this draw Australia won the Bledisloe Cup for the first time in its history. Such was the excitement over this that the team were presented with the Australian Honour Cap, the first time it had been awarded since 1914.

Dooney had already been honoured with the captaincy of an Australian XV against the All Blacks at the Brisbane Exhibition Ground. In a hard-fought match the All Blacks came out ahead by eleven points to six.

In 1936 Dooney returned to Toowoomba and captained both Queensland and then Australia. Appointed captain for the 1936 tour of New Zealand, great things were expected of Dooney and the team, maybe even defeating the All Blacks on their home turf. Heading for New Zealand, he was the first ever captain of Australia to come from Queensland to lead an overseas tour. It was a disaster. In the team's first match against Auckland, Dooney damaged his ribs – an injury he aggravated later – and it wasn't just Dooney, as several other key players went down injured with him. With so many players out, the Australians lost seven of their ten matches in New Zealand.

Dooney's 1937 season was dogged by ill-health and injury, which contributed to a serious loss of form and several humiliating defeats by the South Africans: an Australian XV by 36-3, Toowoomba XV by 60-0 and a Queensland XV by 39-4.

The 1938 season saw his form return and he was selected to play against the touring All Blacks in three tests. The first was played on 23 July at the Sydney cricket ground. Australia went down by nine points to twenty-four, Max Carpenter kicking three penalties. The second test was played on 6 August at the Exhibition Ground, Brisbane. Despite a second half fight back Australia lost again by fourteen points to twenty, Max Carpenter scoring two tries, kicking a conversion and a penalty, and Paul Collins grounding a try. Dooney made his final test appearance on 13 August at the Sydney cricket ground. Australia was once again defeated by six points to fourteen, Mac Ramsay grounding a try and Dooney kicking a penalty and scoring his only points in test rugby.

It was a fine career. He played in five tests and captained his country. He represented Queensland between 1931 and 1938 running out for them on twenty-seven occasions (sixth most capped player for the state, scoring 38 points).

When the war came, Dooney took a commission into the Royal Australian Air Force serving as a flying officer. He was posted to the second Aircraft Delivery Unit RAF, stationed in the Middle East. On 29 October 1942 he was involved in a mid-air collision but managed to bail out successfully, becoming a member of the exclusive Caterpillar Club. Alas his luck didn't hold and on 12 January 1943 he vanished while flying a Kittyhawk in the Magrun area of Libya. Reported missing, he was never seen again.

Edwin Sautelle Hayes is remembered on the roll of honour, panel 123, in the commemorative area of the Australian War Memorial and column 277 on the Alamein memorial. He left a widow, Jacqueline.

411327 Flight Sergeant Francis Ebsworth Hutchinson
Australia
Four tests
460 Squadron Royal Australian Air Force
Died 4/5 January 1943, aged 25
Lock

Played for his country having left school only the year before

Frank Hutchinson was born on 27 December 1917 in Armidale, New South Wales. He was one of three sons born to Arthur Shields and Mary Wilson Hutchinson of North Sydney. He was educated like his brothers at North Sydney Boys High School and the Shore School, Sydney, where he first got to handle a rugby ball and played in the first XV. On leaving school he went up to Sydney University (1935-9) where he was selected for the first XV and represented the university on 74 occasions. Even at the tender age of 15 Frank was an imposing sight: six foot two tall and fourteen stone he looked older than his years. He played his club rugby for Norths (Northern Suburbs Rugby Club, formed in 1900 from the merger of the Pirates and Wallaroos clubs). He formed a close bond with his brother Eric and they played together in the second row for the Norths, Sydney University and New South Wales.

He so impressed the selectors during the inter-state matches that he was selected to play lock during their 1936 tour of New Zealand. He had only left school the year before. Although Hutchinson missed the first match against Auckland (the Wallabies losing by five points to eight) he was selected to play in the second against Wanganui. A hard-fought match, the Wallabies eventually came out on top by twenty-two points to twelve. It was to be one of only two games they won on the tour. This was followed by a match against the impressive Hawke's Bay. Hawke's were known for their physical approach to the game and it was going to be a real tester for the young Hutchinson. Despite playing well the Wallabies went down by twenty points to fourteen, Bill McLaughlin getting a try down and kicking a penalty. Despite the score, Hutchinson played so well he was selected for the first test.

The test was played on 5 September at Athletic Park, Wellington, in front of 30,000 fans. Given their form it was expected to be a walkover for New Zealand. However Australia played better than their critics had expected, eventually going down by only eleven points to six, Bill McLaughlin grounding a try and Ron Rankin kicking a penalty.

Selected for the second test on 12 September at Carisbrook, Dunedin, the outcome was different, with the All Blacks beating the Wallabies by thirty-eight points to thirteen. There had been some hope as Australia was up thirteen-eleven at half time. Owen Bridle and Bill McLaughlin scored a try each with Ron Rankin kicking two conversions and a penalty. Due to an injury picked up during the game against Southland, Hutchinson wasn't selected for the final test against the New Zealand Maoris, which Australia won by thirty-one points to six.

Hutchinson failed to be selected for the 1937 international season due to an injury. However this gave his brother Eric an opportunity and he turned out in two tests against South Africa.

The New Zealand All Blacks toured Australia in 1938. As well as playing for New South Wales against the All Blacks Frank was selected for the national side once again. The first test was played on 23 July at the Sydney cricket ground. In quite a one-sided affair the All Blacks took the game by nine points to twenty-four. Max Carpenter kicked three penalties. Dropped for the second test, Hutchinson was back for the third. The match was played on 13 August at the Sydney cricket ground, the Wallabies going down six points to fourteen in a rather drab affair. The All Blacks returned to New Zealand undefeated. It was to be Hutchinson's final test.

Hutchinson joined the Royal Australian Air Force during the war. After training as a navigator he joined 460 Squadron serving with Bomber Command in England being based in RAF Binbrook in Lincolnshire as part of 1 group. Equipped with Lancaster bombers Mk I and II, Hutchinson was shot down and killed on 4 January 1943 returning from a raid on Essen by a German night fighter. He was flying in Lancaster Mk I, W4274 (AR-B & UV-B). It was his sixth raid. His crew was made up of H.G Brooks (pilot), H.P. Gray (flight engineer), J.H. Watson (second pilot), R.T. Lonsdale (bomb aimer), E.J. Fletcher (wireless operator), and K.J. Harris (rear gunner).

460 Squadron flew the most number one group raids and suffered the highest losses of all the Australian squadrons. Frank's brother Eric was to die twenty-three days later on 27 January 1943. The surviving brother Bill remembered the losses well, 'It caused a great trauma in the family, particularly for my grandmother. My father carried their little photographs in his wallet his whole life, but never talked about them.'

A packet from the authorities arrived at the Hutchinsons' home some time later. It contained one pair of rugby boots and one pair of rugby shorts. There was a folded blazer too, with an Australian crest and the embroidered year '1936'. Frank had taken his Wallabies blazer to war. He must have been proud of it.

Frank is buried in the Uden War Cemetery Noord-Brabant, Netherlands, joint grave 4.G.6-7.

Uden War Cemetery.

403602 Sergeant Eric Hutchinson
Australia
Two tests
Royal Australian Air Force
Died 27 January 1943, aged 26
Lock

'Pat the beloved…He died for victory in War and in Peace.'

Eric Ebsworth Hutchinson was born on 26 September 1916 at McMahon's Point, a harbour suburb of the lower North Shore of Sydney, Australia. He was one of three sons born to Arthur Shields and Mary Wilson Hutchinson. He was educated at North Sydney Boys High School where he first learned to throw and run with a ball before going up to North Sydney University (1939-40). In 1935, aged 19, he turned out for the Northern Suburbs in Sydney as a second row lock, forming part of the team that won that season's championship. It was considered even then that he was destined for great things.

Eric formed a close sporting relationship with his brother Frank (born a year apart). They played together during the mid- to late-1930s in the second rows for Norths, Sydney University (Frank was there between 1935 and 1939) and the New South Wales Waratahs. Eric played for the Norths on 34 occasions and a further 80 times for the university (Francis played on 74 occasions for the university) and 7 times for Manly.

The 1937 season was a good one for Eric. He was selected to play for New South Wales and then made two test appearances for Australia. His brother Frank had made his debut for Australia in 1936 at age 18, touring with the Wallabies in New Zealand. Eric got his opportunity against South Africa (the Springboks) due to Frank being injured and not being able to take part. The match was played on 26 June 1937 at Sydney cricket ground in front of 33,000 enthusiastic supporters. Zero–three down at half time Australia came out fighting in the second half, but they still went down five points to nine. Cyril Towers, who also captained the side, got a try down and kicked the conversion.

Eric turned out again against South Africa on 17 July again at the Sydney cricket ground. South Africa dominated the first half taking a 6-26 lead. The second half was a different matter with Australia fighting back hard. However they still felt short going down 17-26. Aub Hodgson, Jack Kelaher and Frank O'Brian got a try each, Ron Rankin kicked a conversion and two penalties. It was Eric's final test.

On leaving university Eric joined the Royal Australian Air Force, signing up on 3 February 1941. After training Eric was posted to 452 squadron and travelled to England with them. There is a family story about the two brothers meeting up in Lincoln while Eric and Frank were serving in England. The brothers had been reprimanded for not saluting a British officer. The point was made, 'For Christ's sake, if you can't salute the man, salute the uniform.' His words were not lost on them. A short while later the brothers had walked out of a local pub having had a few to drink when they spotted two senior officers approaching them. Instead of saluting them they turned and saluted the store dummies in a nearby uniform shop instead. Once again they were up in front of their commanding officer. We can only guess what was said.

Eric was back in Australia in June 1942, the squadron equipped with Spitfires and sent to Batchelor Airfield in the Northern Territory in 1943. The squadron's orders were to defend Darwin against the marauding Japanese as part of No.1 Wing Royal Australian Air Force. It was while deployed on these duties that Eric was killed in an accident on the 27 January 1943. A report on the accident concluded the following:

RAAF Serial No. A58-73: Mid-air collision 1800 hrs on the 27th January 1943 over Coomalie Creek with another Spitfire, RAAF Serial No. A58-55, during practice section attacks on USAAF B-24s at an altitude of 2,000 to 3,000 feet. Yellow 2 (Eric) collided with the port main plane of Yellow 4 and Eric's tail was broken off. Eric's Spitfire was last seen spiraling inverted and tailless to the ground from 1,500 feet. Sergeant Eric Ebsworth Hutchinson was killed. Yellow 4 made an emergency forced landing at Batchelor at 1820 hrs and the pilot, Sergeant H.W. Stockley, was not injured. A land party reached the crash site at 1200 hrs on the 28th January 1943, some 15 miles away.

Eric was buried in the Adelaide River war cemetery, grave RC12. His family had written on his head stone, 'Pat the beloved…He died for victory in War and in Peace.'

Frank Hutchinson had been killed in action with 460 Squadron only a few weeks before Eric on 4 January 1943.

Bill the surviving brother was stopped from serving overseas due to the deaths of his brothers. It upset him for the remainder of his life. He would later work as a solicitor in Tenterfield. During the 1950s Arthur Hutchinson, their father, wrote to the government asking for financial assistance to see his sons' final resting places. The request was turned down. The news devastated their parents and the situation haunted them to their dying day that they could not afford to visit their sons' graves.

The Hutchinsons' names now stand out on an honour roll in the Australian Rugby Union's headquarters. Two among the seventeen Wallabies to have been killed during two world wars.

NX 59997 Sergeant Russell Lindsay Frederick Kelly
Australia
Seven tests
3 Anti-Tank Regiment, Royal Australian Infantry
Died 25 December 1943, aged 34
Position 8

Repatriated to Australia to die on his own soil

Russell Lindsay Frederick Kelly was born on 5 November 1909 at Murwillumbah, New South Wales. He was the son of Frederick Augustus and Annie Sarah Kelly of Strathfield, New South Wales. He was educated at Sydney Boys High School and Canterbury Boys High School, where he first learned his rugby skills and was, even in those days, seen as a future international.

On leaving school he went to work for the Commercial Banking Company of Sydney Ltd. Kelly was surprisingly fast for a large man, 6ft 1in, 14st 3lbs (90kg), and had been a decent athlete, winning many track events. He played his club rugby for Norths, Drummoyne, Wests and Waratahs making over 100 appearances for these sides. He also played for New South Wales against Queensland (seventeen times), Victoria and South Africa.

He made his first appearance against a touring side when he turned out against the New Zealand Maoris in 1935. The Maoris All Blacks were led by the rugby great George Nepia. They played exciting rugby and were very popular. In many ways they helped stop the mass defection of Australian fans towards rugby league.

Kelly was selected for the 1936 tour of New Zealand. He played lock for the first couple of matches but it didn't seem comfortable. For the tests he was moved to the back of the scrum.

The first test took place on 5 September 1936 at the Athletic Park, Wellington. Despite Australia being six points to five up at half time, New Zealand fought back, finally taking the match by eleven points to six. Bill McLaughlin got a try down and Ron Rankin kicked a penalty. Despite being on the losing side Kelly played well and was praised for his aggressive play.

Kelly was selected for the second test, played on 12 September at Carisbrook, Dunedin. Once again Australia was up at half time, thirteen points to eleven. However in the second half the All Blacks ran amok winning by thirty-eight points to thirteen. Owen Bridle and Bill McLaughlin got the ball down and Ron Rankin kicked two conversions and a penalty.

WESTERN SUBURBS R.U.F.C.
1ST. XV. RUNNERS UP 1937.

R. Kelly, T. Pauling, W. McLaughlin, J. Smallwood,
D. McMaster, W. Rogers, V. Miller, S. Wogan,
H. Button, L. Anderson, T.C. Barnes, A.L.Vincent,
B. Bissaker, G. Anderson, P. Collins.

Despite the heavy loss, Kelly once again acquitted himself well and was selected to play against the New Zealand Maoris on 23 September at the FMG Stadium, Palmerston North. This time it was Australia that ran amok, defeating the Maoris by six points to thirty-one. Jack Kelaher, Mac Ramsay, and Vic Richards got a try down each and Doug McLean scored a hat-trick. Ron Rankin kicked three conversions while Mike Gibbons and Russell Kelly kicked one each. They were Kelly's first international points. Ron Rankin also kicked a penalty. Kelly had used the tour to establish his position in the side.

During South Africa's 1937 tour he was on the winning side when New South Wales punished the Springboks by seventeen points to six. They were the only club side to beat the mighty South Africans during their tour. But on 26 June 1937 at the Sydney cricket ground in a very hard-fought match the South Africans finally triumphed by five points to nine. Cyril Towers got the ball down for the Wallabies and then kicked the conversion.

The second test took place, again at the Sydney cricket ground, on 17 July. By half time Australia was down by twenty-six points to six. However they fought back hard in the second half closing the gap, but not quite enough to take the match, going down by seventeen points to twenty-six.

The New Zealand All Blacks toured again in 1938 and once again Kelly was selected as part of a Wallaby side to oppose them. The 1938 All Black side were considered one of the best ever to tour Australia. Kelly had already had a taster when they crushed New South Wales by twenty-eight points to eight. In fact the All Blacks didn't lose a single match or test throughout their tour. The first test took place on 23 July 1938 at the Sydney cricket ground. In front of 32,000 fans Australia were comfortably defeated by nine points to twenty-four. Max Carpenter kicked three penalties. In the second test, played at the Exhibition Ground, Brisbane, Australia came back from being 3-13 down at half time, to eventually lose by fourteen points to twenty. Several commentators at the time said it was the best encounter between the two sides they had ever witnessed. Max Carpenter got down two tries and Paul Collins one more. Carpenter also kicked a conversion and a penalty.

This was to be Kelly's final international match. Despite being selected for the third test he was forced to pull out due to a thigh strain.

Kelly enlisted into the ranks of the 3 Anti-Tank Regiment, Royal Australian Infantry during the Second World War and was shipped out to the Middle East. He was seriously wounded and captured by the Germans during the battle of Tobruk in 1942, his bravery earning him a mention in despatches. He spent some time as a prisoner before being part of an exchange and shipped back to Australia in 1943. Kelly never fully recovered from his wounds despite several major operations and died at the Concord Repatriation Hospital Sydney on Christmas Day 1943.

He is commemorated at Sydney War Cemetery, memorial reference P.C.8. He was a member of Lodge Bankers (Masonic) who conducted a Masonic Service at the graveside.

The Sydney War Memorial.

QX13648 Bombardier Winston (Blow) Ide
Australia
Two tests
2/10 Field Regiment, Australian Imperial Forces
Died 12 September 1944, aged 29
Centre

As part Japanese, his father was interned in Australia as an enemy alien

Winston Phillip James Ide, whose nickname was 'Blow', was born on 17 September 1914 in Sydney, one of four sons (Harry, Taki and Roy) born to a Japanese silk printer Henry Hideichiro Ide, and Clara, of Northbridge, New South Wales. His father had come to Australia in 1894, becoming naturalized in 1902.

Ide was educated at North Sydney Technical High School. All four brothers played in the school's first XV. He played for Northbridge juniors before turning out for Northern Suburbs whom he represented on seventy-eight occasions.

In 1935 he made his debut as centre for New South Wales against Victoria. In the following season he was selected again and played against Victoria and

Ide can be seen here seated on the bottom row, third from the right.

twice against Queensland. In 1937 Blow moved to Brisbane, following his father into the textiles industry, and joining the GPS club (founded in 1887).

In 1938 Blow was selected to play for Queensland against New South Wales when Dooney Hayes pulled out of the game. Queensland won by seventeen points to nine. He played well and kept his place for the remainder of the Interstate Series.

The All Blacks toured in 1938. Blow missed out on the first test which Australia lost by nine points to twenty-four and it looked like he was going to miss out on the second and third tests too. However he got lucky when Wally Lewis was forced to withdraw from both tests – Ide was selected to replace him, playing inside centre. The second test took place on 6 August 1938 at the Exhibition Ground, Brisbane. Australia went down fourteen points to twenty. Max Carpenter grounded two tries and Paul Collins another. Carpenter also kicked a conversion and a penalty. The third and final test took place on 13 August 1938 at the Sydney cricket ground, Australia going down by six points to fourteen, Mac Ramsay getting a try and Dooney Hayes kicking a penalty.

It was Blow's last appearance for Australia but that was more due to bad luck than lack of talent. Queensland winning the Interstate Series brought Ide's name to the fore and he was selected for the Wallabies tour of Great Britain in 1939. But by the time the team reached Britain aboard the *Mooltan*, war had been declared and the tour was called off. They visited Twickenham, enjoyed a party at the Savoy, and went to Buckingham Palace to shake hands with the king and queen. They then returned home, zig-zagging to avoid enemy U-boats, and on the way managed one match against a Bombay XV. They won easily, but it gave those players who had not represented Australia abroad the right to be called international players.

On reaching Australia Blow joined the Australian Infantry and after training was posted to the 2 / 10th Field Regiment, Eighth Division. He continued to play rugby turning out for GPS, Brisbane, Queensland and the Australian Infantry. He sailed with his regiment to reinforce the garrison at Singapore.

His father was already a prisoner of the Japanese in Malaya which is quite ironic as he was also interned in a camp at Hay in New South Wales as a suspected enemy alien.

To everyone's shock Singapore fell to the Japanese, the biggest surrender in British military history. Among the prisoners taken was Blow Ide. He was imprisoned at the infamous Changi prisoner of war camp before being one of thousands forced to work on the Burma–Siam railway where he remained for three years and was lucky to survive.

Australia

In 1944 the Japanese decided to move hundreds of their prisoners to Japan to work as slaves in the coal mines. Blow was one of 1,318 prisoners of war shipped out on 4 September 1944 onboard the hell-ship *Rakuyo Maru*. Convoy HI-72, with thirteen ships, was first attacked at 2am on 9 December 1944 near Haanan Island by the US submarine *Growler*, which managed to sink an escort ship. It was attacked again at 5.30am, this time by the US submarine *Sealion*, which managed to torpedo a tanker, a freighter and the *Rakuyo Maru*. The prisoners onboard the *Rakuyo Maru* began to jump over the side into the sea or took to the life boats. At 6.15 the USS *Gower* attacked and depth charges were fired at it. These depth charges exploded among the survivors causing many casualties. Sinking slowly, some of the prisoners returned to the ship. However as it was soon clear the ship was lost they returned to the sea around 5.30pm. Blow Ide was seen in the sea and his comrades tried to get him aboard one of the life boats, but Blow refused to climb in shouting, 'I'm staying here ... In any case, I can swim to Australia if I have to.' Blow was never seen again, one of 1,159 prisoners that died that day. Sixty-three prisoners were later saved by the US submarine *Pampanito* and a further forty-four by the US submarine *Sealion*. The US submarines *Barb* and *Queenfish* rescued a further thirty-two survivors and the Japanese pulled 136 more out of the sea.

Although initially reported as missing, Blow was assumed to have died on 12 September 1944. He is commemorated on the Labuan Memorial, Malaysia, Panel 2.

The Labuan Memorial, Malaysia.

England

**Pilot Officer Prince Alexander Obolensky
(The flying Prince, The Flying Slav, Obo)
England
Four tests
504 Squadron Royal Air Force
Died 29 March 1940, aged 24
Wing**

King Edward VIII: 'By what right to you play for England?'
Prince Obolensky: 'I played for Oxford University, Sir.'

Prince Alexander Sergeevich Obolensky was born on 17 February 1916 in Petrograd (now Saint Petersburg) Russia. He was the son of Prince Sergei Alexandrovich Obolensky, an officer in Tsar Nicholas II Imperial Horse Guards and his wife Princess Lyubov (née Naryshkina). Given their connections to the Russian royal family they were forced to flee Russia after the Bolshevik takeover in 1917. Seeking sanctuary in England they settled in Muswell Hill, London.

PRINCE OBOLENSKY

Alexander was educated firstly at the Ashe School, Etwall, before going up to Trent College in Long Eton Derbyshire in 1929. It was here that his flair for rugby was first noticed. Selected for the school's first XV in 1932 he was part of the team that had an unbeaten run scoring 539 points while conceding only 22 and in one season alone scoring forty-nine tries. He also played football for Chesterfield FC, Leicester FC and Rosslyn Park FC. Awarded a college exhibition to read PPE he went up to Brasenose College Oxford during the Michaelmas term of 1934. He finally qualified with a fourth-class degree in 1938. His lack of academic prowess might be explained by the amount of time he spent on the rugby field, winning two blues for Oxford as a wing three-quarter. He was awarded his first blue for Oxford in 1935, his freshman year. He missed the 1936 (Cambridge victory) match due to injury but was selected for the 1937 Varsity Match, an Oxford victory by seventeen points to four.

England

Chosen to play for England against New Zealand on 4 January 1936 at Twickenham, his selection was controversial as he was still a Russian national. However as he had agreed to become a British citizen, his selection was confirmed (he actually became a British citizen a few weeks after the match in March 1936). During his pre-match introduction Edward VIII, aware of the controversy, asked Obolensky, 'By what right do you play for England?' Obolensky replied, 'I attend Oxford University, Sir.'

The match was played in front of 73,000 cheering spectators. Obolensky didn't disappoint, scoring two tries, both in the first half. Sidestepping the New Zealand fullback Mike Gilbert and then outpacing him he grounded his first try. However it was his second try that was to go down in rugby history. Taking the ball on the right wing he cut across the field at speed touching down just inside the left corner flag. In so doing he had managed to outpace the entire New Zealand defence and run three-quarters of the length of the field. It was regarded then and still is by many now as the greatest try England ever made. England went on to take the match by thirteen points to zero (Hal Sever scored the third try and Peter Cranmer dropped a goal). It was the first time England had defeated the All Blacks (and would be the last until 1973) and the match passed into folklore. *The Times* described it as 'a remarkable match, with a still more remarkable result.' (There is a Pathé News item of the match which can be viewed on YouTube.)

Obolensky was to go on to win three further caps during the 1936 Five Nations matches, including against Wales on 18 January 1936 at St Helen's, Swansea, zero-zero draw, and against Ireland on 8 February at Lansdowne Road, Dublin, a victory for Ireland by six points to three, Aidan Bailey and Vesey Boyle touching down for Ireland and Hal Sever getting the points for England. Obolensky played his final international against Scotland on 21 March 1936 at Twickenham, England coming out on top this time by the narrow margin of nine points to eight. England's try scorers were Reggie Bolton, Peter Candler and Peter Cranmer. Wilson Shaw got the ball down for Scotland and Ken Fyfe kicked a conversion and a penalty.

Obolensky's England career might have ended but not his rugby career. He toured Argentina with the British Lions in 1936 and made seven appearances for the Barbarians (invitation only) between 1937 and 1939 touching down three tries. Included within these matches were two Edgar Mobbs Memorial matches against the East Midlands (see *Into Touch* by the same author). In 1936 he also contributed to the book *Be Still and Know: Oxford in Search of God*. He graduated from Oxford in 1937. In 1938 he was appointed a Knight of St John.

Obolensky was commissioned into the Royal Air Force Auxiliary in 1938 and was called up for active service in 1939. Training as a fighter pilot he was posted initially to 615 Squadron at RAF Kenley before joining 504 Squadron, flying Hurricanes. Despite his wartime duties he still found time for rugby. At Richmond in December 1939 he played in the joint English and Welsh side that beat a joint Irish and Scottish side by seventeen points. In March 1940 in Cardiff he also played in the English side that beat the Welsh by eighteen points to nine, all the proceeds from these matches going to charity.

The squadron was transferred to Digby flying from Martlesham Heath Airfield, Suffolk. Obolensky was killed on 29 March 1940 while flying Hurricane L1946 when his aircraft overshot the runway and dropped into a ravine breaking his neck (some reports say he was doing aerobatics at the time). Obolensky had previously confided to friends that he found landing the hardest part of his training. Obolensky was the first English International to fall in the war. He is buried at Ipswich's war cemetery, Section X.H. Grave 423. The inscription on his grave reads

*HIS UNDAUNTED SPIRIT AND ENDEARING QUALITIES LIVE
FOR EVER IN THE HEARTS OF ALL WHO KNEW HIM*

The 'Obolensky Lecture' is given annually on the subject of rugby football, and at Twickenham there is a suite named *Obolensky's* in his honour. There is also a statue of him in Cromwell Square Ipswich and a building was named after him at his old school, Trent College. The 'Prince Obolensky Award' is presented annually by the Prince Obolensky Association at Rosslyn Park FC.

Second Lieutenant Paul Cooke
England
Two tests
Oxfordshire and Buckinghamshire Light Infantry
Died 28 May 1940, aged 24
Scrum Half

Died protecting the BEF on the beaches of Dunkirk

Paul Cooke was born on 18 December 1916 in Marylebone, London. He was the son of William and Dora Cooke of Slough, Buckinghamshire. He was educated at St Edwards School, Oxford. It was here that Cooke learned to play and excelled at rugby establishing himself as a solid Scrum Half and playing in the school's first XV. On leaving school he went up to Trinity College Oxford. His talent on the rugby field was quickly recognized and during the summer of 1936 he was selected to tour South America as part of a British representative side, taking the honours in all ten matches he played. During this time he played with his friend and fellow Oxford University player Alexander Obolensky known as 'the Flying Prince', who was also to die in the war on 29 March 1940. Returning to Oxford he was selected for the Oxford University team winning his blue against the old enemy Cambridge on 8 December 1936 at Twickenham. Playing in poor weather, Cambridge finally came out the victors by six points to five. Despite the loss Cooke represented his university against Cambridge again the following year on 7 December 1937 winning his second blue. This time it was a different matter and it was Oxford that took the honours by an impressive gap of seventeen points to four, Cooke scoring two tries, the last one coming in the final minutes of the match. As one paper later put it, 'Finally in the last minutes of all Cooke rubbed it in by picking up a loose ball and scoring a fifth try.'

On leaving Oxford, Cooke decided on a career in banking, playing his club rugby for Richmond. In January 1939 his talent

Rugby Football Union
Twickenham

2D.   2D.

OFFICIAL   PROGRAMME

ENGLAND v. WALES
SATURDAY, 21st JANUARY, 1939
Kick-off 2.30 p.m.
PRICE TWOPENCE

was finally recognized and he was selected to make his international debut for England against Wales at Twickenham. The match took place on 21 January 1939 in the most atrocious conditions. Over 70,000 fans attended and England were captained by Herbert Toft. Both sides struggled but England finally came out the victors by three points to nil, Derek Teden (who was later killed with 206 Squadron RAF on 15 October 1940) having got a try down. Cooke did well, one report stating, 'Cooke lost no chances to open up an attack on the blindside.'

He was selected again to play against Ireland on 11 February 1939, once again at Twickenham. It was to be a special occasion for the English side and Twickenham as it was the fiftieth game to be played there and hopes were high for a good result. The team was captained once again by Herbert Toft. However, as ever, the Irish had their own plans. For once the weather was good and this seemed to inspire the Irish as they outplayed the English in almost every department, taking the match by five points to nil with a try by John Irwin and a conversion by Harry McKibbin. *The Times* later said of Cooke, 'Cooke and his partner were gallant enough in defence but in attack and counterattack... found the worrying pace of the game too much for them.'

ENGLAND 1939

England 0 - Ireland 5 - Twickenham - 11th February 1939

J C H Ireland (Referee) R S L Carr R M Marshall J K Watkins J T W Berry H D Freakes G E Hancock R H Guest D E Teden
H F Wheatley   J Heaton   H B Toft (Captain)   T F Huskisson   R E Prescott
G A Walker   P Cooke

England

It was to be Cooke's last international match for England. He was however later selected for the Barbarians Traditional Easter tour of Wales. As with so many players of the time we shall never know how well Cooke could have done with his talent. I feel he would almost certainly have regained his England spot at some point. But it wasn't to be. Hitler invaded Poland and we were quickly at war.

Keen to get involved, Cooke joined the ranks of the Oxfordshire and Buckinghamshire Light Infantry in September 1939 before being commissioned as a second lieutenant on 9 March 1940. He was shipped out to France to join his regiment, First Battalion serving with the British Expeditionary Force (BEF). The First Battalion were a territorial battalion and originally went to France as part of 11th Infantry Brigade, 4th Infantry Division later becoming part of the 143rd Infantry Brigade 48th Division. After a period of quiet better known as the 'phoney war', the Germans launched their offensive in May 1940. Fearful of being outflanked, surrounded and captured, the BEF began their historic fighting retreat towards Dunkirk, the rearguards' main objective being to give the army isolated on the beaches of Dunkirk a fighting chance of getting away and back to England. As part of this operation on 26 May 1940 the Ox and Bucks made a stand on the Ypres–Comines canal. Outnumbered and outgunned the battalion held back the Germans' advance for a vital two days before being forced to pull back. Alas it was here on 28 May 1940 that Second Lieutenant Cooke who was serving with 'D' company was killed while getting a Bren gun into action from the window of a house. The regiment was eventually given the order to pull back on 29 May. When they were finally picked up off the beaches at Dunkirk the battalion had suffered over 300 casualties.

He is buried in British Plot, Grave 1, of the Commines (Konam) Communal Cemetery.

Pilot Officer Bryan (Brian) Black
England and British Isles
Fifteen tests
England Ten tests/British Isles Five tests
601 Squadron Royal Air Force (Auxiliary Air Force)
Died 29 July 1940, aged 33
Lock

Won two gold medals in the two- and four-man bobsleigh

Brian Henry Black was born in South Africa on 27 May 1907 the son of Francis and Elizabeth Black (later of South Kensington, London). He was educated at St Andrew's Grahamstown, Eastern Cape, South Africa, before going up to Brasenose College Oxford as a Rhodes scholar. Soon playing rugby for his university he won his blue in 1929 playing lock against Cambridge, Oxford taking the honours. He also began playing his club rugby for Blackheath (whom he also played cricket for). On leaving Oxford he established himself as a solicitor.

PROGRAMME

Rugby International
at Twickenham

SATURDAY, FEB. 22

ENGLAND
v.
FRANCE

Kick-Off 3.0 p.m.

Remaining as a lock, he made his debut for England against Wales on 18 January 1930 together with eight other players making their test debuts (J.G. Askew, A.H. Bateson, J.W. Forrest, P.D. Howard, D.A. Kendrew, F.W.S. Malir, M. Robson and W.H. Sobey) in the Five Nations Championship. The match was played at the National Stadium, Cardiff. England played well and were ahead at half time 0-3 eventually taking the match 3-11. Black managed a penalty goal and a conversion.

He made his next appearance for England against Ireland, again in the Five Nations, at Lansdowne Road, Dublin. Despite being 0-3 up at half time Ireland went on to take the match by 4-3.

It wasn't until 22 February 1930 that Black made his home debut, turning out for England against France at Twickenham. Up 6-5 at half time England eventually won the match by 11-5, Black kicking a conversion, Jim Reeve, Joe Periton and Matthew Robson making the tries. Scotland were next, played on 15 March 1930 once again at Twickenham. The teams drawing 0-0.

England

Because of his consistent form Black was selected for the British Lions tour of Australia and New Zealand. Although a personal triumph for Black, being the Lions top scorer with a total of 82 points (three tries, twenty-six conversions and seven penalty goals), the tour didn't go so well. The first match was played on 21 June 1930 in Carisbrook, Dunedin. In front of a crowd of 27,000 Great Britain were ahead at half time 0-3 finally taking the match 3-6. It was to be their only

BRITAIN VICTORIOUS IN THE FIRST RUGBY TEST.

international victory of the tour. The second match was played at Lancaster Park, Christchurch, on 5 July 1930. In front of 30,000 people New Zealand took the honours 13-10. On 26 July Great Britain played New Zealand at Eden Park, Auckland, this time the crowd numbering over 40,000. New Zealand won by 15-10. Black managed to make his first score kicking a conversion. The next test was played on 9 August 1930 at the Athletic Park, Wellington, once again in front of another large crowd of over 40,000. New Zealand took the honours once again, winning 22-8. Again Black was on the score sheet, kicking a conversion. It was Black's last appearance in New Zealand. He made one further international appearance, against Australia on 30 August 1930 at the Sydney Cricket Ground, which Australia won 6-5.

Black next played in the Five Nations in 1931. His first match was against Wales, played at Twickenham on 17 January 1931. The match was drawn 11-11 with Black scoring two penalties. His next match was played on 14 February 1931 against the Irish at Twickenham in front of a crowd of 60,000. Black scored the only try and conversion. Despite this England went down 5-6. On 21 March 1931 Black was at Murrayfield, Edinburgh, to take on Scotland. With a crowd exceeding 75,000, Black made two conversions and scored a penalty. Despite his best efforts England went down 28-19.

On 6 April 1931 Black played against France at the Stade Olympique Yves-du-Manoir, Paris. Black kicked a conversion, but England went down 14-13. It had been a disastrous Five Nations.

In 1932 Black only turned out once, on 19 March against Scotland at Twickenham. This time England managed to take the match 16-3, Black scoring one of the four tries.

He played his final match for England against Wales on 21 January 1933 at Twickenham in front of 64,000 excited fans. England lost 3-7.

He played fifteen international matches for England and Great Britain. He scored thirty-four points making two tries, eight conversions, and four penalties. He was on the winning side on four occasions, on the losing side on nine occasions, and played in two draws.

Black did not only excel at rugby. A fine and accomplished all-round sportsman, he represented Great Britain in 1937 in the two-man Bobsleigh in Cortina, northern Italy, together with the Australian Frederick McEvoy. Although South African-born he qualified, as many did at the time, by virtue of having gone to university in England (McEvoy qualified the same way). Defeating teams from Italy (silver) and Switzerland (bronze) the British team managed to take the gold. Moving quickly to St Moritz he also took gold for the four-man bobsleigh defeating Germany (silver) and the USA (bronze). His crew were made up of Frederick McEvoy, David Looker and Charles Green.

At the outbreak of the war Black took a commission into the Royal Air Force becoming a pilot officer. He was killed together with Pilot Officer Geoffrey Edward Moon RAFVR on 29 July 1940 when his Avro Tutor K3287 flying from the RAF flying training school at RAF Upavon span into the ground and exploded at Chilmark, Wiltshire. He is buried in Upavon Church Cemetery, Wiltshire, Row E, Grave 4.

Pilot Officer Ernest Parsons DFC
England
One test
10 Squadron Royal Air Force
Died 14 August 1940, aged 27
Full Back

There is no greater love than to lay down one's life for one's friends

Ernest Ian Parsons was born on 24 October 1912 in Linwood, Christchurch, New Zealand. He was educated at Christchurch Boys' High School and Canterbury University College. Deciding on a career in the Royal Air Force he left New Zealand to join up, which he did on 6 November 1939 in Kent.

Parsons was selected to play for England against Scotland in the Calcutta Club. The match was played on 18 March 1939 at Murrayfield. They didn't know it at the time but it was to be the last major pre-war match. Scotland had already lost their first two matches, away to Wales and Ireland, and was determined to try to make up for it against England. England had beaten Wales 3-0 before going down to Ireland 5-0. With England playing the better rugby they eventually came out ahead by six points to nine, England kicking three penalties all scored by Jack Heaton to Scotland's two tries touched down by William Murdoch and Wilson Shaw. The Scottish journalist Sandy Thorburn later wrote, 'Although it was disappointing to lose because of three penalties, the result was fair, for a disciplined England pack dominated the game and a spark of enterprise in their backs would have seen Scotland routed.'

Tragically six players from this match were to die during the war. From Scotland, George Roberts, 1943, Tom Dorward, 1941, and Donald Mackenzie, 1940, and from England, Derek Teden, 1940, and Robert Mackenzie Marshall, 1945.

Training as a pilot, Parsons joined 10 Squadron (motto: *rem acu tangere* – to hit the mark) who were part of Four Group based at RAF Dishforth, flying Armstrong Whitworth Whitley bombers. The squadron made leaflet drops over Berlin on 1/2 October 1939 (becoming the first squadron to fly over the city during the war); one of the four aircraft failed to return. The squadron's first bombing raid took place on 19/20 March 1940, when eight Whitleys, each carrying mixed bomb loads of 1,500lbs, attacked the German minelaying seaplane base at Hörnum on the island of Sylt. They suffered no losses.

With Italy's entry into the war the squadron flew from the advanced base of the Channel Islands to bomb the Fiat works at Turin. One aircraft failed to return.

On the night of 13 / 14 August the squadron took off from Abingdon to attack the Fiat aero-engine works at Turin, flying Whitley Mark V P4965 ZA-Hs. Opposing them were night fighters, Fiat CR 42s from 150o *Gruppo*. One of their pilots, Capitano Giorgio Graffer, scrambled so quickly that he was

A Whitley bomber.

wearing only a pair of tennis shorts. He attacked 10 Squadron over the target at 01:55. He later described his attack on Parsons' Whitley in his own words:

> ... *the night of August the 14th I was ordered to scramble over Turin. I took off with a wingman against enemy planes signalled by the AA defence. Each of us started to search independently and I was lucky to discover an enemy from the flames coming from its exhaust pipes. I attacked it from astern and it returned fire hitting my engine. I tried again to shoot at it from below but my guns refused to fire and the engine was losing oil. Considering that my plane was close to ending its life I decided to try to collide with the enemy plane and save myself with the parachute. I flew over the enemy but the stream from its airscrews overturned my plane and I failed my first attempt, so I flew on the side of the enemy plane and I hit its empennages with my airscrew. My plane spun down and I abandoned it. I acted in this way because I'm convinced that the plane that I was flying had been given to me with the purpose of using it against the enemy and my action although quite dangerous if well conducted was not suicidal.*

Badly shot up by Graffer's attack which left one engine out of action and severe damage to the starboard aileron, Parsons still managed to fly his crippled Whitley across France. However while trying to land on the beach near Dymchurch Redoubt on the Kent coast, the weakened aileron broke off and the Whitley plunged into the sea. Despite this, three of the crew still managed to escape, observer Sergeant Chamberlain, wireless operator Sergeant Marshall and air gunner Sergeant Sharpe. Unfortunately the two pilots were not so lucky and both were killed on impact. They were Pilot Officer Parsons and co-pilot Sergeant Alfred Norman Campion. Their bodies were eventually washed onto the French coast and buried in Boulogne's Eastern Cemetery in the Pas-de-Calais, plot 12, row D, grave 6. This was the first successful night interception by an Italian fighter during the war. Graffer was awarded the *medaglia di bronzo al valor militare*. For his bravery in getting the crippled plane back Parsons was decorated with the Distinguished Flying Cross (DFC), a well-earned award.

England

Pilot Officer Derek Teden
England
Three tests
Royal Air Force (Auxiliary Force), 206 Squadron
Died 15 October 1940, aged 24
Prop

Scored a try on his debut for England

Derek Edmund Teden was born on 19 July 1916 at Highgate, London. He was the son of Frank Edmund Teden and Zilla née Collingridge. He was educated at Lord Williams School in Thame before moving on to Taunton School. While there he didn't really shine at rugby and struggled to get a permanent place in the first XV. It wasn't until after he left school and turned out for Old Tauntonians that he impressed a scout from Richmond. Joining Richmond his form quickly improved. He turned out for Middlesex and was selected by the Barbarians to play in the annual Mobbs memorial match on 4 March 1937 against the East Midlands (which they lost by thirteen points to three). In the same year he was also selected as a reserve by England for their match against Ireland.

Despite his rising success it wasn't until 1939 that Teden made the breakthrough into the England side, chosen by the selectors to play against the Welsh pack on 21 January 1939 at Twickenham. The match was played in appalling conditions and despite Wales's best efforts England were the better side and came out ahead by three points to nil. The only try being scored by Derek Teden. *The Times* later commented,

'What greater honour could have befallen a new front row man like D.E. Teden than to join in such a scrummaging triumph.'

After such a fine debut Teden was selected again, this time to play against Ireland on 11 February at Twickenham (England's fiftieth match at Twickenham). Unfortunately Ireland spoiled the party playing the better rugby and coming out ahead by five points to nil. Teden played well, making a try although it was disallowed, but Ireland were the better team on the day and deserved the victory. The final match of the 1939 season came against Scotland at Murrayfield on 18 March. Once again Teden was selected for the match. In a scrappy game England eventually came out on top by nine points to six – thanks to three successful penalty kicks from Jack Heaton the Calcutta Cup was theirs again.

A Lockheed Hudson – the type of plane that Teden was flying when he and his crew disappeared.

It would be the last time Teden would wear the England shirt. However he did don the Black and White hooped jersey of the Barbarians for their Easter tour of Wales. He also turned out for Richmond and Rosslyn Park.

With the outbreak of war Teden was already a pilot officer with the Royal Auxiliary Air Force, having been commissioned on 27 October 1938 into 604 (County of Middlesex) Squadron. In 1940 he transferred to 206 Squadron Coastal Command. In early 1940 the squadron moved to St Eval in Cornwall to guard the south-west approaches from German attacks. On 15 October 1940, Teden left St Eval flying a Lockheed Hudson to carry out a reconnoitring mission. Teden and his crew were never seen again despite a full search being launched. His crew consisted of: Sergeant James Steel, Pilot Officer John Lionel De Keyser and Sergeant William Kent.

Teden is commemorated on Runnymede Air Forces Memorial, panel ten. He is also remembered in Thame on the Lord Williams School memorial board.

England

Major Henry Rew
England
Ten tests
Four tests (British Lions)
7th Royal Tank Corps RAC
Died 11 December 1940, aged 34
Prop

His bravery began the collapse of the Italian position in Egypt

Henry Rew was born on 11 November 1906 in Exeter. He was the son of Henry Godfrey and Ethel Mary Rew. He was educated at Exeter School (together with his brother Robert Godfrey) where both brothers played in the first XV playing wing three quarter. Henry made his debut for Exeter RFC in 1924 as a wing three quarter at the tender age of 17 (his brother Robert also played for Exeter). A powerful runner and a useful kicker he became a regular with the Exeter side, later also being selected to play for Devon.

Deciding on a career in the army he joined the Tank Corps in 1928. He quickly established himself with the Army XV playing in the annual service tournament. He also turned out for Blackheath. His form must have been consistent and good because he was quickly spotted by the England selectors. Rew was to go on to play in ten tests between 1929 and 1934.

He made his debut for England in the Five Nations against Scotland on 16 March 1929 at Murrayfield in front of a crowd of 80,000. Thomas Harris, Stephen Meikle, Tony Novis and Edward Richards also made their debut in the same match. Despite being three up at half time, England went down by twelve points to six, the England tries coming from Meikle and Novis.

Despite the loss, the selectors kept faith with Rew and he was chosen for the XV against France at the Stade Olympique Yves-du-Manoir on 1 April 1929. Three-eight up at half time England went on to take the match by six points to sixteen. It was the last match of the season.

Between 3 April 1926 and 27 December 1934 Rew turned out for the Barbarians on nineteen occasions.

In the 1930 season Rew missed the first two matches, against Wales on 18 January (England victory 3-11) and against Ireland on the 8 February (England lost 4-3). He was however selected to play against France at Twickenham. The match was played on 22 February in front of a full house of 70,000 enthusiastic fans. England was only just ahead at half time, 6-5. However England had the better of the second half coming out ahead 11-5. Twickenham was the venue of the next and final match of the Five Nations, against Scotland, played on 15 March. Unusually it was drawn nil all. It was the last match of the Five Nations, England having come out top by a whisker.

In June of the same year Rew was selected to travel on Great Britain's (Lions) tour of New Zealand. He played in eleven games and all four tests. The first test was played in Dunedin on 21 June 1930, Great Britain getting the better of New Zealand and winning by three points to six. A few weeks later, on 5 July, this time at Christchurch, the New Zealanders had their revenge defeating Great Britain by thirteen points to ten. At Auckland on 26 July the result was the same, New Zealand coming out ahead, this time by fifteen points to ten. The final test was played in Wellington on 9 August. By now the New Zealand pack had the measure of England and defeated them 22-8, although it could have been a lot more.

During the 1931 Five Nations, Rew was selected to play in three of the four games. His first appearance was against Wales at Twickenham on 17 January. Despite being ahead 8-6 at half time the match ended as an 11-11 draw. His next match was against Scotland at Murrayfield on 21 March. Scotland played the better rugby and came out winners by twenty-eight points to nineteen. He was next chosen to play against France at the Stade Olympique Yves-du-Manoir on 6 April. To everyone's surprise France took the match by fourteen points to thirteen despite being down 5-4 at half time.

Rew wasn't selected again until the 1934 Five Nations. He turned out against Wales at the National Stadium, Cardiff, on 20 January, England taking the honours by zero points to nine. Next was Ireland at Lansdowne Road, Dublin, on 10 February. Once again it was England that took the match by a convincing three points to thirteen. Rew's final international came against Scotland at Twickenham on 17 March. Once again it was an English victory by six points to three. England won the Championship, the Triple Crown and the Calcutta Club.

Promoted to major, Rew was posted to the Western Desert with the 7th Royal Tank Corps (RTC). On the night of 9/10 December 1940 Major Rew led the Matilda Tanks of A Squadron with B Squadron in support and D Squadron in reserve against the fortified position of Nibeiwa which was held by the Italians. Because of the speed of the attack the Italians were caught completely by surprise. The tanks had travelled 800 metres before the first shells fell among them. The Matilda's two-pound shot easily penetrated the Italian M11/39 tanks. Soon twenty-eight Italian tanks were burning on the battlefield, their crews shot to pieces. Rew and his tanks were quickly inside the Italian position. The Italian and Libyan garrison resisted the attack with great determination, attacking the British tanks with hand grenades and machine guns. Even the Italian c.o. General Maletti was killed attacking a British tank with a machine gun. By 10.40 it was all over. The Italian and Libyan troops suffered 4,157 casualties for a British loss of 56 men killed and 27 tanks disabled or broken down. Alas one of the casualties was the gallant Major Henry Rew. He didn't die in vain however. The success at Nibeiwa began the collapse of the Italian position in Egypt.

He is buried in the El Alamein Cemetery, grave reference XXXI.H.8.

D/MX 31440 Master at Arms William Luddington
England
Thirteen tests
Royal Navy (HMS *Illustrious*)
Died 10 January 1941, aged 46
Prop

First player to ever score a point at Murrayfield

William George Ernest Luddington was born at the Ferndale Hospital in Aldershot on 8 February 1894. He was the son of William George Ernest and Jessie Luddington. William's father was a soldier and posted to Devonport shortly after William's birth. Probably because of the naval influences around him William enlisted into the Royal Navy. His talent for rugby quickly became apparent. He played for Devonport Services, United Services and the Devon County XV. In 1921 he was selected to play for the Royal Navy. He went on to play for the Navy on sixteen occasions playing against both the Army and the Royal Air Force on eight occasions. He eventually went on to captain the Navy XV. Assisted and guided by engineer Commander E.W. Roberts, who was an England selector, his game was focused and improved. Not surprisingly he was soon called up to play for England.

He made his debut in the Five Nations against Wales on 20 January 1923 at Twickenham in front of a crowd of 40,000 excited fans. England were the better side overall and took the match 7-3 (3-0 at half time), Leo Price grounding a try and Alastair Smallwood dropping a goal. The papers said of Luddington's first appearance, 'Luddington did not spare [himself] or anybody else in the mauls.'

Luddington next turned out against Ireland on 10 February 1923 at Welford Road, Leicestershire, in front of a crowd of 20,000. England won the match by the convincing margin of twenty-three points to five. Len Corbett, Cyril Lowe, Leo Price and Alastair Smallwood scored tries, Geoffrey Conway kicked two conversions, and Dave Davies dropped a goal.

He next appeared against Scotland on 17 March 1923 at Inverleith, Scotland, in front of the Duke of York. 30,000 fans turned out for the occasion. In a hard fought and close match England took the game by six points to eight. With Scotland in front and only seconds to play, England managed get across the line and score a second try levelling the match. Luddington was now on the spot in every respect. He was up to the challenge and stepping up scored the all-important conversion and winning the match. As the *Times* rugby correspondent later reported, 'All the more honour for Luddington for refusing to let his knees or his toe wobble… at the critical moment.' Alastair Smallwood and Tom Voyce scored a try each and England retained the Calcutta Cup.

Luddington made his final appearance in 1923 against France on 2 April at the Stade Olympique Yves-du-Manoir in front of a crowd of 35,000. England won the game by three points to twelve. Once again Luddington kicked a conversion. Geoffrey Conway and W.W. Wakefield grounded tries and Dave Davies dropped a goal. England took the Grand Slam.

Selected to play in the Five Nations again during the 1924 season he first turned out against Wales on 19 January at St Helen's, Swansea, in front of a crowd of 35,000. England took the match by nine points to seventeen. Carston Catcheside scored two tries, Harold Jacob, Harold Locke and Edward Myers one each. Conway kicked a conversion.

His next match was against Ireland on 9 February at Ravenhill, Belfast. Fifteen thousand turned out to see England defeat Ireland by three points to fourteen. Catcheside grounded two tries, Len Corbett and Richard Hamilton-Wickes one further try each. Conway kicked a conversion.

Against France a few weeks later on 23 February at Twickenham in front of 40,000 cheering fans, England took the match by nineteen points to seven. Jake Jacob grounded three tries, Carston Catcheside and Arthur Young getting one each. Geoffrey Conway kicked two conversions.

On 15 March England defeated Scotland by a convincing nineteen points to zero, again at Twickenham. Forty thousand fans went home happy. Catcheside, Myers and Wakefield scored all the tries. Conway kicked three conversions and Myers dropped a goal. It was England's second Grand Slam in as many years.

Selected to play in the Five Nations again in 1925, his first match was against Wales, played on 17 January at Twickenham in front of a crowd of 35,000. England continued with their winning ways beating Wales by twelve points to six. Hamilton-Wicks, Harold Kittermaster and Tom Voyce scored the tries and Rex Armstrong kicked a penalty.

Against Ireland at Twickenham on 14 February, England only managed a 6-6 draw despite being 6-0 up at half time, Alastair Smallwood getting both tries for England. It was a sign of things to come. Against Scotland on 21 March at Murrayfield, England lost for the first time in three seasons, 14-11 despite being 5-8 up at half time. The Edinburgh pubs were full that night. Richard Hamilton-Wicks and Wavell Wakefield grounded tries for England and Luddington kicked a conversion and a penalty.

Of all the matches Luddington was to play it was this one that he is best remembered for and the only time he was on the losing side. It was the first international played at Scotland's new stadium at Murrayfield. Early in the game Luddington successfully took a penalty and thus entered the history books as the first player ever to score international points at the new Scottish stadium. Quite an accolade.

England restored their winning ways against France on 13 April at the Stade Olympique defeating France by eleven points to thirteen. However, many thought the score closer than it should have been, especially considering England were up 5-13 at half time. Hamilton-Wickes and Wakefield scored the tries. Luddington kicked two conversions and one goal from a mark.

Now into his thirties, International rugby was, Luddington felt, a business for 'younger men'. He played his final international for England against Wales on 16 January 1926 at the National Stadium, Cardiff. The match was drawn 3-3, Wakefield grounding a try for England.

During his international career Luddington was on the winning side on ten occasions, drawing twice and only ever losing one match. He kicked five conversions and one penalty. Although his international career was over he continued to play for the Navy and even found time to meet, fall in love with, and marry Vera Jackson on 17 February 1927 in Plymouth.

During the war Luddington served as a master-at-arms on the aircraft carrier *Illustrious* and saw considerable action while serving on her, protecting the convoys that were carrying desperately-needed supplies to Malta, attacking airfields at Maritza and Benghazi, as well as attacking the Italian Fleet at Taranto, sinking one battleship and seriously damaging two others.

On 10 January 1941 however, HMS *Illustrious* was attacked by a squadron of Junkers 87 Stuka dive-bombers near Sicily. She was hit eight times causing serious damage which would keep her out of action until 1942. During the attack Luddington was killed, together with 125 officers and enlisted men. Ninety-one others were wounded.

Luddington has no known grave and his commemorated on the Plymouth Naval Memorial, panel 56, column 1. He is also commemorated at Twickenham.

The HMS *Illustrious*, pictured in 1940.

The Rev Christopher (Kit) Tanner AM
England
Five tests
Royal Naval Volunteer Reserve, HMS *Fiji*
Died 23 May 1941, aged 32
Wing

The only England rugby international to be awarded the
Albert Medal during the Second World War

Christopher Champain Tanner was born on 24 June 1908 in Cheltenham. He was the son of Maurice Tanner, clergyman and schoolmaster, and Alice. He was educated at Cheltenham College where he played in the first XV. On leaving Cheltenham he went up to Pembroke College, Cambridge. Despite coming with a fine reputation as a quick-running wing, the university, at first anyway, failed to include him. However the Barbarians were not so blind and selected him to wear their famous black and white hooped shirt in the Edgar Mobbs memorial match against the East Midlands on 6 March 1930 at Northampton. (Edgar Mobbs DSO won seven caps for England. He was killed in action on 31 July 1917. See *Into Touch* by the same author.) The match saw a resounding victory for the Barbarians by twenty-two points to six. Tanner excelled, touching down three tries in front of the England selectors. *The Times* later commented, 'the strong and determined running of Tanner had been one of the features of play.'

Selected to play for England, he turned out against Scotland at Twickenham on 15 March 1930. The match was attended by none other than HRH the Prince of Wales (later Edward VIII). The match wasn't a classic and ended in a goalless draw. Scotland retained the Calcutta Cup by default as they already held it. However, far from being criticized, Tanner was praised by *The Times* once again: 'Tanner did his best… and, in fact showed such a power of stride he looked every inch a scorer.'

It was England's last match of the season, and although not their best, they still took the championship. Tanner failed to be selected for any internationals during the 1931 season. However that didn't stop him being selected by the Barbarians. He turned out for their annual Christmas match against Leicester on 26 December 1930, the Barbarians taking the match 6-13.

This was followed up by selection for the Barbarians Easter tour of Wales. Tanner turned out against Cardiff on 4 April 1931, the Barbarians taking the match 9-11, followed by Newport on 7 April, the Barbarians coming out on top again by nine points to eighteen.

Finally, Tanner's talent was recognized by his university and he was given his blue playing for Cambridge against Oxford on 9 December 1930. The match concluded in a three-all draw. So, despite not being selected to play for England, not a bad season.

The 1932 season saw Tanner's international fortunes change for the better. He was selected to play for England against South Africa at Twickenham on 2 January 1932. Although not the favourites, England still played poorly going down 0-7. However once again Tanner's contribution was a good one, one paper noting, 'He [Tanner] got in one run that really raised the rather despondent crowd.'

Despite this defeat the selectors kept faith with Tanner and he was chosen to play against the Welsh at Swansea on 16 January 1932. Things went no better, as England went down 12-5 despite the

efforts of the backs including Tanner. Eric Coley got the ball down for England and Bobby Barr kicked a conversion.

Tanner was in the team that travelled to Dublin to take on the mighty Ireland on 13 February 1932. Expectations were not great: Ireland had not been defeated in three seasons. Despite this, England pulled of a surprise victory by eight points to eleven. Don Burland got the try and kicked a conversion and two penalties.

Tanner next turned out against Scotland at Twickenham on 19 March 1932, the last match of the season. In a one-sided match, England came out on top by sixteen points to three. Tanner managed his debut try for England. His try was later reported as, '…he then went at full tilt for the corner, turning in a bit to hand off Macpherson just before he crossed the line.'

The Calcutta cup had been returned to England. Carl Aarvold scored two tries, Brian Black one and Kit Tanner one. Don Burland kicked two penalties.

Alas the Scotland match was to be the last Tanner played for his country. He turned out on two further occasions for the Barbarians in 1933, against the East Midlands and Newport, both victories, which meant he had never played on a losing side while representing the Barbarians. He also turned out for Richmond and Gloucestershire.

Tanner was ordained in 1935, becoming the curate at Farnham Royal for two years, becoming the curate of St Mary de Lode in Gloucester, and then in 1939 becoming the rector at Haslemere. During this time (1937) he married Eleanor Rotherford at St Leonard's in Chesham, Buckinghamshire. With the outbreak of the war he became a chaplain with the Royal Naval Volunteer Reserve.

Tanner was posted as a chaplain to the battle cruiser HMS *Fiji*. In 1941 the ship was tasked with preventing the Germans invading Crete. Interestingly, her captain at the time was the former Navy rugby captain and Welsh international Captain Peveril William-Powlett who would win the DSO for his actions on 23 May 1941.

HMS *Fiji* was under almost continual attack from the Luftwaffe, mostly Stuka dive-bombers. The fleet had already lost HMS *Juno*, HMS *Greyhound* and HMS *Gloucester* to similar attacks. During the attacks, HMS *Fiji* had an estimated 350 bombs dropped towards her before she was finally hit at approximately 7pm on the 23 May 1941. The order to abandon ship was given when the *Fiji*,

HMS *Fiji*.

listing at thirty degrees, received more bombardment and flipped onto her side. They managed to get some life-rafts off but nowhere near enough for all the survivors. Kit Tanner was seen cheering up the crew and tending to the wounded. He also brought them mugs of hot chocolate and sandwiches. In Captain William-Powlett's words, 'His cheerful influence infected the bridge and by God, I needed cheering up.'

The destroyer HMS *Kandahar* came to assist and began to pick up survivors, however she was also attacked and had to pull away, promising to return after dark. Their captain ordered the crew to stick close together and await the return of the destroyer. Four hours later it did return. Unfortunately many men had succumbed to the sea by then. Kit Tanner was, as ever, a tower of strength, helping and calming the men whenever he could. He got the men singing musical hall songs and some others a little bawdier. He assisted one seaman who had had his arm blown off. He must have made a difference as the sailor survived.

Scrambling nets were thrown over the side of the ship and the survivors began to climb. However, many of the crew were too exhausted or too badly wounded to make the climb. Kit Tanner, who had already climbed onboard the *Kandahar* and was helping to pull men onto the ship, on seeing men struggling in the sea jumped back into the sea to help, getting people onto the scrambling net and helping them up. He did this time and time again, diving back into the sea and pulling men to safety. Despite his level of fitness, this continual exertion proved too much. Climbing on board for the last time he collapsed onto the deck and died. Thirty-four officers and 500 men were saved out of *Fiji*'s complement of 700. It is estimated that Kit personally saved over thirty of them.

For his actions on that day Kit Tanner was posthumously awarded the Albert Medal. The Albert Medal, instituted by Queen Victoria in 1866 for saving life at sea, was one of the rarest awards of the war. The *London Gazette* of 28 April 1942 reported:

> *The Reverend Christopher Champain Tanner, Temporary Chaplain, R.N.V.R., H.M.S. Fiji, who, when H.M.S. Fiji was sunk in the Battle of Crete, stayed to save the wounded men from the sick bay, and was one of the last to leave the ship. While in the water he spent himself in helping men to rafts and floats and, when the rescuing ship came up, in bringing over to her disabled men and such as could not swim. At length only one man remained to be brought across. Despite his exhaustion Mr. Tanner made a last effort to save him. He brought him across and saw him safely on board. But when hauled up himself he died within a few minutes.*

Kit Tanner was the only England international to be awarded the Albert Medal throughout the war and as such deservedly sits alongside Arthur Leyland Harrison, the only England international to be awarded the Victoria Cross.

Kit was buried at sea and is commemorated on the Portsmouth Naval Memorial, panel 60, column 3. He is also commemorated at his old school, Cheltenham College, at Pembroke College, Cambridge, and there is a Rood cross at St Christopher Church Haslemere dedicated to his memory.

England

Vice Admiral Norman Wodehouse
Royal Humane Society Silver Medal/Order of Striped
Tiger of China
England
Fourteen tests
Royal Navy (*Robert L. Holt*)
Died 4 July 1941, aged 54
Forward

Led England to their first ever Grand Slam

Norman Atherton Wodehouse was born on 18 May 1887 in Basford, Nottingham. He was the son of the Reverend Frederick Wodehouse and his wife Alice. Destined for the navy he was sent first to the Royal Naval School, Lee-on-Solent and then to the Britannia Royal Naval College as an officer cadet in 1902. He was promoted to midshipman in 1903 and in 1906 to acting sub-lieutenant, the rank being confirmed the following year in 1907. It was also in 1907 that he won his first rugby cap for the navy, the navy overcoming the army. Promoted to lieutenant in 1908 he became a fixture in naval rugby from 1909 until 1914 taking seven caps overall. During this time he also represented the United Services, as well as turning out for the Barbarians against Leicester (draw).

In 1910 Woodhouse was selected to specialize as a gunnery officer and also selected to play for England. His debut was to come against France on 10 March 1910 at the Parc des Princes. England came out on top three points to eleven. Harry Berry grounded one try and Arthur Hudson two more. Fred Chapman kicked a conversion. Wodehouse played well and became a permanent member of the England team until 1913.

In 1911 he played in all four of the Five Nations matches. Against Wales on 21 January 1911 at Swansea, England went down by fifteen points to eleven. Next came France at Twickenham on 28 January, England outclassing France and winning by an impressive thirty-seven points to zero. Woodhouse scored his debut try for England during this match. Next was Ireland at Lansdowne Road on 11 February. As a result of the score against France much was expected; they were to be disappointed going down three points to zero. On 18 March England were pitted against Scotland at Twickenham, England winning the match thirteen points to eight, Wodehouse scoring his second try for England. It was the final match of the season.

53

The following season, 1912, he was selected once again for all four of the Five Nations games. The first game was against Wales on 20 January at Twickenham. England played well and came out on top 8-0. Twickenham was the venue again for the match against Ireland on 10 February. Again England dominated the match coming out winners 15-0. On 16 March he was selected to play against Scotland at Inverleith. He was also made captain, a position he kept until he retired from international rugby. Given their form, England had high hopes, but Scotland had other ideas taking the match eight points to three. The final match of the season was played against France on 8 April at Parc des Princes. Wodehouse, captaining the England side, helped them take an eight points to eighteen victory.

Remaining as captain for the 1913 season, Wodehouse was selected to take on South Africa at Twickenham on 4 January 1913. Despite the match being a 3-3 draw at half time, South Africa finally took the match 3-9.

Selected to play in the Five Nations for the final time he retained his captaincy. Against Wales at Cardiff on 18 January England came out convincing winners by zero points to twelve. France were next on 25 January at Twickenham. It was a convincing England victory by twenty points to zero. Lansdowne Road and Ireland were next on 8 February. England outplayed Ireland winning by four points to fifteen. Wodehouse's final international was played against Scotland at Twickenham on 15 March. In front of a crowd of 25,000 England won three-zero. As a result an undefeated England claimed their first ever Grand Slam. *The Times* later commented, 'such success as the English teams had this season could only have been achieved under the best leadership [Wodehouse's].'

Serving throughout the First World War Wodehouse won the Royal Humane Society Silver Medal when in 1915 he dived over the side of his ship to save a drowning seaman who had fallen into the sea from a different ship. In the same year he was also promoted to lieutenant commander. During the Battle of Jutland Wodehouse served as a gunnery officer on the battleship *Revenge*, serving with the 1st Battle Squadron under the command of Captain E.B. Kiddle, second in line behind HMS *Marlborough*, flying the flag of Vice-Admiral Sir Cecil Burney. *Revenge* first engaged the light cruiser SMS *Wiesbaden*, eventually helping to sink her. She then attacked SMS *Derfflinger*, hitting her five times and landing a further shell on SMS *Von der Tann*, damaging her. *Revenge* had fired 102 shells from her main guns and 87 from her 6-inch guns. She also fired one torpedo and engaged Zeppelin L11 with her anti-aircraft guns.

After the war Wodehouse was promoted to full commander. He was posted to China as fleet gunnery officer, a tour of duty that earned him the Chinese Order of the Striped Tiger.

In 1923 he married Mrs. Theodosia Frances Swire, née Boyle. They had two sons.

He was promoted to captain in 1926 and attended the Imperial Defence College's senior officers' war course. He then commanded the cruiser HMS *Ceres* and HMS *Calypso*. Between 1931 and 1934 he commanded the Royal Naval College, Dartmouth. He became a flag captain in the Mediterranean on HMS *Barham* before becoming head of the British military mission in Portugal and did much to stop Portugal going the same way Spain had, falling under the influence of the Spanish Fascists.

He then became aide-de-camp to King George VI, being presented with the Companion of the Order of the Bath.

A few months before the Second World War, Wodehouse was promoted to rear admiral. His final appointment was command of the naval dockyards on Gibraltar. He eventually retired from the navy on 8 May 1940.

However the needs of war are many and he returned quickly to duty becoming a commodore (2nd Class) with the Royal Naval Reserve. Attached to HMS *Eaglet* in Liverpool, Wodehouse finally took command of convoy OB337, which sailed on 20 June 1941. This convoy was heading for southern Africa and Wodehouse decided to sail with it on board the armed merchantman the *Robert L Holt*, bound for Warri in Nigeria and commanded by Master John Alexander Kendall. On 4 July 1941 the *Robert L Holt* was intercepted by the German U-boat the *U69*, commanded by Korvettenkapitän Jost Metzler north-west of the Canary Islands. Instead of using a torpedo, the submarine surfaced and opened fire on the merchantman at 04.36. Despite being armed it was a one-sided affair and the *Robert L Holt* was sunk at 06.50 after the U-boat had fired 102 high explosive rounds and 34 incendiary rounds from the deck gun, 220 rounds from the 20mm gun and 400 rounds with the MG34. The master, the commodore, 41 crew members, 8 gunners and 5 naval staff members were lost, including Wodehouse. The *U69* was lost later during the war.

Wodehouse is commemorated on the Liverpool Naval Memorial, panel 1, column 1.

Captain Vivian Gordon Davies
England
Two tests
Royal Artillery
303 Searchlight Battery
Died 23 December 1941, aged 41
Fly Half

Prisoner of War in the First World War, died in the Second

Vivian Gordon Davies was born on 22 January 1899 at The Grove Durham. He was the son of Horatio Gordon Davies and Blanche Frances Madeline Wind. He was first educated at the Bow prep school (now Durham School) where he first played rugby, establishing himself as a fly half with the school's first XV. He then went up to Marlborough College where he was again in the first XV. He played in 1914 (aged 15 and the youngest member of the XV), 1915, and 1916 when he captained the side.

On leaving school in 1916 Davies took a commission as a second lieutenant in the 15th Battalion Durham Light Infantry (DLI). In 1917 he was posted to the front.

In 1918, on 27 May, despite having advanced for weeks the DLI suddenly faced a massive German attack and was forced to retreat. In two days of fighting, 15 DLI lost over 450 men killed, wounded or missing. Among the missing was Second Lieutenant Vivian Gordon Davies. This must have been a harrowing time for his parents as many men reported missing were alas dead. However on 12 September 1918 his parents learned that he was in fact a prisoner of war and being held at the German camp at Strialsund Dänholm, an island in northern Germany.

On being repatriated to England he continued his military interest joining the 7th County of London Regiment (TA), before transferring to the Royal Artillery AA Battalion Special Reserve and being promoted to lieutenant on 13 February 1937.

He continued with his rugby too. He played for the Harlequins for four years and captained them over seventy times. He also played for Durham County and Surrey.

On 22 June 1922 he married his girlfriend Gwen, his sister Primrose being a bridesmaid. The couple eventually moved to Flat 7, 50 Sloane Street, London.

England

Davies won two caps for his country. Playing fly half the first was against Wales in the Five Nations on 21 January 1922 at the National Stadium Cardiff. The match was a disaster for England who lost 28-6, Wales downing eight tries to England's two, and Wales taking the championship.

He wasn't recalled to play for England again for three years. Selected to play against New Zealand at Twickenham on 3 January 1925 England went down again, this time by eleven points to seventeen. It was to be Davies' final international match.

During the war he served as a captain with the Royal Artillery, 303 Search Light Battery. He was taken ill and died aged 42 on 23 December 1941. His remains were cremated at Mortlake Crematorium where he is commemorated on a screen wall memorial, erected by the Commonwealth War Graves Commission, situated adjoining Mortlake Cemetery, on panel 4.

Pilot Officer Hubert 'Trilby' Freakes
England
Three tests
RAFVR (Royal Air Force Ferry Command)
Died 10 March 1942, aged 28
Full Back

'War cut short the most promising of careers'

Hubert Dainton Freakes (known as Trilby to his friends, a nickname he picked up at Cambridge) was born on 2 February 1914 in Durban in South Africa, the son of Benjamin and Blanche. He was educated at Maritzburg College where his ability on the sporting field was quickly recognized and he was made captain of both the rugby XV and cricket XI. He was also a fine athlete. Leaving school in 1930 at 16 he went up to Rhodes University in Grahamstown. During this time he continued to play both rugby and cricket at provincial level for Eastern Province. In completing his education in South Africa he won a Rhodes scholarship to Magdalen College, Oxford, in 1936. Six weeks later he found himself winning his blue, being selected to take on Cambridge at the annual varsity match at Twickenham on 8 December 1936 – a remarkable achievement in itself. Playing fullback in driving rain, Cambridge played the better rugby taking the match by six points to five. Despite this loss Freakes acquitted himself well working hard and playing hard to the end of the match. The following year, on 7 December 1937, Freakes was once again included in the Varsity team, taking his second blue. This time it was a different matter, with Oxford taking the honours by seventeen points to four. One newspaper reporting the match said, 'In the capacity of a full back disguised as a centre, Freakes made his selection appear a stroke of genius.'

Called up for international duties, Freakes was selected for England against Wales, played on the 15 January 1938 in Cardiff. It was a historic match, being the fiftieth time the two sides had met. Played in gale force winds in front of 40,000 fans, Wales were by far the better side and took the match by fourteen points to eight. Peter Candler and Hal Sever scored a try each and Freakes managed to kick a conversion. Allen McCarley and Idwal Rees got a try each for Wales and Viv Jenkins kicked one conversion and two penalties. There was singing in the valleys that night. *The Times* appreciated his performance and said of him, 'Freakes in his first international game as a full back was subjected to the fiercest of tests.' It was to be his only international that season.

England

For the 1938/9 season he was made captain of Oxford and once again played in the Varsity match at Twickenham. The match was played on 6 December 1938 with Cambridge taking the honours by the narrow margin of eight points to six. *The Times* later stated, 'As the game went on, Freakes may have regretted his decision to play at full back rather than centre, where last year his tackling alone was decisive.'

Playing for the Harlequins he continued to impress and was given another opportunity to play for his country the following season. Again his opening match was against Wales. The match was played on 21 January 1939 at Twickenham. This time it was England's turn to take the honours with a 3-0 victory, a hard-fought match with a surprisingly low score. Derek Teden grounded the try. *The Times* were complimentary once again: 'H.D. Freakes at full-back was a splendidly sound defender and ready enough to turn defence into attack.'

Impressed by his performance, Freakes was selected to play in the next international against Ireland. Once again a historic occasion as it was the fiftieth time England and Ireland had met. It was also to be Freakes' last international. The match took place on 11 February 1939 at Twickenham. Ireland were the better team on the day and eventually beat the English pack by five points to nil, John Irwin scoring the try and Harry McKibbin kicking the conversion. Despite Freakes' best efforts the Irish finally broke through, scoring the winning try.

On 18 July 1939 Freakes joined the Royal Air Force Volunteer Reserve as a pilot officer before being promoted to flying officer on 12 February 1941. Attached to the Royal Air Force Ferry Command his duties were basically to collect aircraft from their factories and deliver them to their RAF squadrons. Many of these squadrons were in Canada and the USA so he chalked up hundreds of flying hours in a variety of aircraft. During the war the Ferry Command delivered over 9,000 aircraft to various units and squadrons.

On 10 March 1942 he was flying Hudson Bomber V8995, and shortly after takeoff it was seen to lose control and spin into the ground, exploding on impact at Honeybourne airfield in Worcestershire. Freakes and all his crew were killed.

He is buried in Evesham Cemetery, grave reference 1338.

Freakes was also a fine cricketer and made ten first class appearances for the Eastern Province and The Rest. See *The Coming Storm* by the same author.

One of his crew members at the time was Sergeant John Edward Baartz of the Royal Australian Air Force, aged 21, of Queensland, Australia. They are buried side by side. The rest of the crew consisted of Sergeant Thomas Francis Dale RAFVR, an air gunner from Middlesbrough, aged 28, and Sergeant Ernest Watson, a wireless operator/air gunner, 19 years old, from Selby.

Pilot Officer Lewis Booth
England
Seven tests
10 Officer Training Unit
Died 25/26 June 1942, aged 33
Wing Three Quarter

'The most natural player I ever saw'

Lewis Alfred Booth was born on 26 September 1909 at Horsforth, Leeds, the son of Alfred and Amie Helena. He was educated at the Malsis School, Crosshills, North Yorkshire (closed in 2014) between 1920 and 1922, the first few years of the school's existence (his son and grandson were also later educated there). While there he excelled at sports especially rugby, playing in the school's first XV as a wing three quarter, a position he maintained for the rest of his rugby career. He played his club rugby for Headingley.

Booth made seven international appearances for England, between 1933 and 1935. He made his debut for England against Wales on 21 January 1933 in the Home Nations Championship, in front of a crowd of 64,000 at Twickenham and captained by Carl Aarvold (later the judge at the trial of the Kray twins in 1965). England were 3-0 up at half time thanks to a try from Walter Elliott. However Wales came back strongly in the second half finally taking the match 3-7 thanks to a try and a drop by Ronnie Boon (better known as Cocky, he was also a first class cricketer and played eleven first class games for Glamorgan). It was the first time a Welsh XV defeated England at Twickenham, ending the so-called 'Twickenham bogey'.

Booth next turned out against Ireland, again at Twickenham, on 11 February 1933, this time under the captaincy of Tony Novis (Novis served with the Leicestershire Regiment during the war, rose to the rank of lieutenant colonel, commanded the 1st battalion in Normandy, was wounded twice and won the Military Cross). Nine-six up at half time, England finally took the honours seventeen-six. It was a memorable match for Booth as he scored his first try. Bernard Gadney (late captain of England) got another, Tony Novis got two down and Edward Sadler (on his debut – later he became a rugby league player) a fifth. Joe Kendrew (he won a DSO and two bars during the Second World War adding a third bar during the Korean War) managed a conversion. Ted Hunt (killed during the fighting at Wong Nai Chong Gap, Hong Kong, on 20

December 1941 while serving with the Royal Engineers) managed a try for Ireland, and Paul Finbarr Murray kicked a penalty.

His next match was against Scotland played at Murrayfield on 18 March 1933. England was captained once again by Tony Novis. The match was a low scoring one with Scotland coming out on top by three points to zero, Kenneth Carmichael Fyfe making the only score with a try. It was to be Booth's final match of the 1933 season.

Booth only turned out once during the 1934 season, playing against Scotland at Twickenham on 17 March 1934 (almost a year since his last game). England were captained by Bernard Gadney. This time it was an England victory. Three-three at half time England went on to take the match six-three. Booth grounded a try as did Graham William Churchill Meikle. Robert Wilson Shaw managed a try for Scotland. It was to be Booth's only match that season.

Booth next turned out against Wales on 19 January 1935 at Twickenham. Captained by Joe Kendrew and in front of 72,000 fans the match was drawn 3-3. Harold Brought kicked a penalty for England and Wilf Wooller managed to run in a try for Wales (Wooller was a prisoner of the Japanese during the war and was lucky to survive the horrors of Changi camp. He later became a broadcaster with the BBC and sports journalist with the *Sunday Telegraph*). Booth next played against Ireland on 9 February 1935, again at Twickenham and again captained by Joe Kendrew. This time England took the honours 14-3 (5-0 at half time). Broughton kicked three penalties and a conversion and Jimmy Giles managed a try. Joseph O'Connor managed a try for Ireland.

Booth played his final international against Scotland on 16 March 1935 at Murrayfield. England were captained by Bernard Gadney. At half time Scotland were 10-4 up and although England came back in the second half, Scotland finally took the match 10-7. Despite losing, Booth did manage a try (some consolation during his final match) the other score being Peter Cranmer who managed to drop a goal. (Cranmer was also a first class cricketer.) For Scotland Ken Fyfe managed a try and kicked two conversions, while Lindsay Lambie managed a further try.

During the Second World War Booth served with the Royal Air Force Volunteer Reserve. Having trained as a navigator he joined No. 1651 Conversion Unit RAF flying out of RAF Waterbeach. At some point during this time he managed to meet and marry Gladys Louise of Huby in Yorkshire and they had several children.

On Thursday, 25 June 1942, the aircraft of the 1651 CU Squadron (RAF), took off at 23.58 for a mission to Bremen in Germany. Booth was the navigator in a Short Stirling (type I, serial number W7442 and code B). Having attacked their target and on their way home Booth's aircraft was attacked and shot down by night fighter pilot Leutnant L. Linke of the II/NJG 2 from Leeuwarden airfield. The Stirling crashed at Waddenzee. There were no survivors. The crew consisted of:

Pilot Flight Lieutenant W.M. Livingston 66541 RAF, Harlingen, E, row 4, grave 4.

Flight engineer Sergeant W. Bennett 613080 RAF, Runnymede Memorial, panel 78.

Observer Pilot Officer A.J. Kenny 47747 RAF, Harlingen, E, row 2, grave 13.

Navigator Pilot Officer L.A. Booth 118627 RAF, Runnymede Memorial, panel 68.

Bomb aimer Pilot Officer F.L. Flynn J/7541 RCAF, Runnymede Memorial, panel 100

WO Ag Sergeant R. Coates 1111952 RAF, Harlingen, E, row 2, grave 12.

Air gunner Pilot Officer J. Graham DFM 47909 RAF, Runnymede Memorial, panel 69.

Booth is also commemorated on the stained-glass window in the chapel of his old school, Malsis, together with fifteen other members of the school that lost their lives.

England

Major Ronald Gerrard DSO
England
Fourteen tests
7th Field Squadron Royal Engineers
Died 22 January 1943, aged 31
Centre

'No man living or dead was braver'

Ronald Gerrard was born on 26 January (some records have it as the 18th) 1912 in Hong Kong. He was the son of William George, an assistant commissioner of police, and Elizabeth Ann. Due to his father's early and unexpected death Ronald left Hong Kong aged 15 and resumed his education at the Taunton School in Somerset. He quickly established himself as a fine all-round athlete, playing in the first XV and first XI. An opening batsman, he headed up the Taunton batting averages on three occasions, his best innings being 123. He excelled at weight-putting, winning the public schools competition in 1929 and 1930. He was a fine shot and excelled at fives, water polo and tennis. He was also a decent soccer player. He went on to make three first class cricket appearances for Somerset losing against Worcestershire, beating Glamorgan and losing once again against Worcestershire (see *The Coming Storm*).

On leaving school he became articled to a Bath firm of civil engineers but kept up his sports, playing club rugby for the Bath first XV and making his debut for them at Plymouth on 11 October 1930. At the tender age of 17 (1930) he was selected to play for Somerset against Gloucester playing centre three quarter. He also captained Somerset between 1933 and 1939. He retained his place in the county XV until the outbreak of the war in 1939.

His speed and energy on the field soon caught the eye of the England selectors and he was given a trial in 1931. It went well and he made his debut against South Africa at Twickenham on 2 January 1932. In front of 70,000 people, England went down by seven points to zero.

He next turned out against Wales in the Four Nations played at St Helen's, Swansea, in front of a crowd of 30,000. Wales took the honours by 12-5.

He next turned out against Ireland at Lansdowne Road, Dublin, on 13 February 1932. This time England managed to take the match eight points to eleven. It was Gerrard's first victory. Don Burland took all the points for England with a try, a conversion and two penalties.

Gerrard made his last international appearance in 1932 against Scotland on 19 March at Twickenham, England coming out on top by sixteen points to three in front of a cheering crowd of 65,000. Carl Aarvold scored two tries, Briand Black and Christopher Tanner a further try each. Burland kicked two conversions.

Gerrard was selected again the following year, 1933, to represent England in the Four Nations. His first match was against Wales at Twickenham on 21 January. In front of a crowd of 64,000 Wales beat England three points to seven despite England being up at half time by three points. Walter Elliot grounded a try for England, Ronnie Boon managed a try and a conversion for Wales.

He next turned out against Ireland, again at Twickenham, on 11 February. England managed the win by seventeen points to six. England scored five tries: Lewis Booth, Bernard Gadney, Tony Novis (captain) who grounded two, and Edward Sadler. Joe Kendrew managed a conversion.

Gerrard next turned out against Scotland on 18 March at Murrayfield. Scotland won by three points to zero thanks to a try by Ken Fyfe. It was his final match in 1933.

The following year the England selectors kept faith with Gerrard and he was selected for the Four Nations once again. His first match was against Wales on the 20 January 1934 at the National Stadium, Cardiff. On this occasion it was England that took the match by nine points to zero, disappointing a crowd of 50,000 mostly Welsh men. Graham Meikle grounding two tries and Tim Warr a third.

Ireland was next, on 10 February at Lansdowne Road. England were victorious, winning by three points to thirteen, Henry Fry putting down two tries and Graham Meikle another. Gordon Gregory kicked two conversions.

Scotland was next at Twickenham, England making it a clean sweep by defeating them six points to three. Lewis Booth and Graham Meikle grounding tries for England.

Gerrard missed playing in 1935 but was selected to play against New Zealand on 4 January 1936 at Twickenham in front of a crowd of 73,000. Six-zero at half time, England finally took the match by thirteen points to zero. Alexander Obolensky got two tries down and Hal Sever one. Peter Cranmer dropped a goal.

Selected again for the Four Nations, his first match was against Wales on 18 January at St Helen's, Swansea. The match was drawn 0-0.

Against Ireland on 8 February at Lansdowne Road, England lost by six points to three despite being three up at half time. Hal Sever scored the try for England.

Gerrard's final international experience came against Scotland on 21 March at Twickenham. England were 9-8 up at half time thanks to tries from Reggie

Bolton, Peter Candler and Peter Cranmer. The scores remained the same and England took the match. Gerrard's final record was eight wins, five losses and one draw.

Gerrard also captained the combined Somerset and Gloucester Counties XV versus New Zealand in 1936. He played twice for Barbarians and was also in their winning squad at the 1934 Middlesex Sevens. He appeared in 45 games for Somerset, 20 as captain.

In 1937 he married Miss Mollie Taylor, a local architect who went on to become the first lady president of Bath Rugby Club.

Having been commissioned into the Territorial Army, he was called up at the beginning of the war, serving with 7 Field Squadron Royal Engineers and rising to the rank of major. Deployed to North Africa he was decorated with the DSO (*London Gazette* 31-12-42) for clearing a minefield while under heavy fire. His actions in hazardous conditions contributed to the Allied advance during the North African campaign. His citation read:

> *Major Gerrard showed the greatest courage and determination in his leadership which was an inspiration to all who saw it. The successful piercing of the enemy fields in this sector was largely due to his personal efforts and example.*

Three months after being decorated, Major Gerrard was killed on 22 January 1943 in action near Tobruk. He is buried in the Tripoli War Cemetery, grave reference 8.E.3.

Lieutenant Commander R. Michael Marshall, DSC and bar
England
Five tests
Royal Naval Volunteer Reserve, HMMGB 2002
Died 12 May 1945, aged 27
Number eight

'we know that death found him unmoved, unhurried, undismayed, with the game for which he had played, as he had always played soundly and honourably won'

Robert Michael Marshall (Mike) was born on 18 May 1917 at Giggleswick School (founded in 1512), North Yorkshire, where he was also educated. He was the son of Robert and Elizabeth. A natural athlete, Marshall excelled at most sports, however it was at rugby they he shone. Playing in the second row he achieved God-like status on the rugby field. On finishing school in 1936 he went up to Oriel College, Oxford, where his reputation as a rugby player preceded him. He achieved his first blue playing for Oxford against Cambridge on 8 December 1936 at Twickenham. Despite Marshall's and Oxford's best efforts Cambridge managed to take the game by the narrowest of margins six points to five. A few weeks later Marshall turned out for the Barbarians taking part in their annual Christmas game against Leicester on 28 December. This time he was on the winning side, the Barbarians taking the match by twenty-eight points to five.

Marshall played his club rugby for Scarborough, joining the club at 16 and becoming their first ever international. However he is probably more famously known for playing for the Harlequins being considered the best forward that ever took the field for the club.

Marshall was again selected to represent Oxford against Cambridge on 7 December 1937. The match was played once again at Twickenham this time in front of King George V. Although Cambridge started the match as favourites they were outmanoeuvred by the Oxford XV who went on to win the game by the comfortable margin of seventeen points to four. He was also selected by the Barbarians to play against Leicester, again in their Christmas fixture against Leicester. The match was played on 28 December 1937. They crushed Leicester 34-0, an outstanding start to the New Year.

England

As would be expected Marshall soon came to the notice of the England selectors and he was chosen to play for England against Ireland on 12 February 1938 in the Home Nations at Lansdowne Road, Dublin. England took the match by thirty-six points to fourteen. Reggie Bolton, Jimmy Giles, Basil Nicholson, Robin Prescott, Jeff Reynolds, Jimmy Unwin all grounded tries as well as Mike Marshall, scoring on his debut. Graham Parker kicked six conversions and a penalty. *The Times* later reported:

> *RM Marshall, a new forward in the second row, was a stupendous success, and that not only because he ran some fifty yards to score the try of the match.*

Marshall was selected to play against Scotland on 19 March at Twickenham. Despite being played in front of the king and queen, this time the result didn't go England's way and they were defeated by Scotland 16-21. Jimmy Unwin got the English try with Grahame Parker kicking three penalties and Jeff Reynolds kicking a dropped goal. In so doing the Scots claimed their first win at Twickenham since 1926, also taking the international championship and the Triple Crown.

Marshall was selected to play for Oxford for a third time in the annual varsity match against the old enemy Cambridge on 6 December 1938. Although it was Oxford this time that started as favourites Cambridge rose to the occasion and defeated Oxford by eight points to six. The following year Marshall was selected to play for England, this time against Wales at Twickenham on 21 January 1939. England took the match by three points to nil, Derek Teden grounding the try. Again *The Times* spoke of him in glowing terms, comparing him to another great Harlequin:

> *Marshall, again, stood out for two breaksaway, the likes of which have not been seen since Wakefield retired.*

Marshall was selected to play against Ireland on 11 February at Twickenham. Ireland pulled of a surprise victory by zero points to five. Marshall made his fifth and final appearance for England against Scotland on 18 March at Murrayfield. This time England took the honours by six points to nine. This victory gave England a share of the International championship. England didn't manage a try, relying on Jack Heaton to kick three penalties.

On 10 November 1939 Marshall joined the RNVR as a temporary sub-lieutenant, being promoted to lieutenant on 1 February 1942 and lieutenant commander in November 1944. During this time he found time to marry Muriel Stella, daughter of the Rev and Mrs P.M. Daubeny of Old House Farm,

Cublington, Bucks (she married Major General Sir Ronald Campbell Penney after Marshall's death). They had two daughters.

Between 25 May 1942 and November 1943 he was commanding officer of HMMGB 607 (MGBs – motor gun boats – were popularly known as 'dog boats'). Stationed at Great Yarmouth, he took part in many operations, often at night and in difficult conditions, and won the Distinguished Service Cross.

On the night of the 24/25 October 1943 a force of over thirty German E-boats attacked a northbound convoy near Smith's Knoll on the Norfolk coast. They were engaged by two MGBs, one commanded by Marshall in 607 and the other by Lieutenant F.R. Lightoller in 603. They quickly sank two E-boats with gunfire before Marshall rammed a third, the S88, which sank. The 607 didn't come out of the action without casualties. So damaged was she that the 603 was forced to tow her back to Yarmouth. Marshall's citation read, 'His aggressive spirit was a fine example to all Commanding Officers of Coastal Force Craft, and is in the finest traditions of the service.' (*London Gazette* 8-2-44)

Marshall's first lieutenant on 607 later recorded his experiences of the man:

> In all situations Mike was an outstanding officer; big, tough, quick-witted, confident, decisive and very thorough and competent. He demanded high performance and got it. He engendered confidence in all serving with him, the officers and men of MGB607 and other members of the flotilla who worked with us. Undoubtedly he was a leader of men. The qualities that earned him a blue for rugby at Oxford and a cap for England were always evident. He was a hard task-master, a great teacher and a great man.

Between 22 November 1943 and November 1944 Marshall was commanding officer of HMMGB 503. It was while in command of the 503 that he commanded the first Bonaparte mission. This mission involved rescuing nineteen souls who had escaped the Germans and needed to be ferried home. Most of the nineteen were RAF aircrew that had been shot down over enemy occupied territory. It was during this time that he was to win a second DSC for bravery. His citation read:

> His first task was to get his ship into reliable running order... a series of serious mechanical breakdowns had undermined the morale of her crew... under Lt Marshall's direction the ship rapidly became operational. After accompanying two operations as an observer... Lt Marshall embarked on a series of 12 faultlessly executed expeditions. Four of these operations were to parts of the North French coast not previously visited; Lt Marshall displayed outstanding skill in locating accurately these new pinpoints,

entering narrow rock strewn channels without hesitation. On one occasion he pressed on and completed an operation of great importance in a north-easterly gale gusting to force 8, under conditions which would have made a less determined officer give up long before reaching the French coast. MGB 503 embarked 100 Allied airmen from a beach in enemy occupied France between January and March 1944. The procedure involved lying at anchor within a mile of enemy watch posts for between two and four hours at a time. The standard of efficiency to which Lt Marshall had trained his surf boats' crews needs no emphasis in view of these figures. By skillful tactics and cool and correct judgment, Lt Marshall avoided detection by enemy sea patrols and convoys indicated by radar and visually on a number of occasions. His high qualities of leadership and seamanship are worthy of recognition.' (*London gazette* 27-3-45)

With the end of the war in Europe MGB 2002 was tasked with a special mission transporting merchant navy officers to Gothenburg to arrange the return of three British merchant vessels. The 2002's normal captain, Jan Mason, was away in London being awarded his own DSC, so Marshall volunteered to assume temporary command for the mission in his stead. On 11 May 1945 MGB 2002 left Aberdeen and was never seen again. Two survivors were found but not Marshall. MGB 2002 had hit a mine cut free by a British minesweeper.

The following obituary was later written by E.H. Partridge in *The Times*:

Others can speak with greater knowledge of a service career, which though brief had already earned signal marks of distinction; but as the name and exploits of Marshall have in a few years taken on at Giggleswick something of a sanctity of legend, I hope I may be permitted a brief tribute to the rare excellence of character which won his assured place in our hearts rather than those athletic gifts which placed him, when little more than a boy, among the great rugby football players of all time. To those of us who have seen him go for the line, a breath taking vision of swift, beautifully balanced power, the exploit which earned him his first decoration came as no surprise. But it was not individual skill which made Marshall essentially great, I have seen no player who could by sheer force of character and the use of a minimum of words so change the adverse fortune of a game. He was not a first class cricketer, but when the team failed he retrieved the game more than once, with a devastating defiant century from low down on the list. As captain of a rugby football side he can have no equal and war claimed him at a time when the greatest honours that the game could offer were well within his grasp. But we shall remember rather the

69

head of school who enjoyed respect accorded to few masters, who ran his prefects with the same silent efficiency as his fifteen, and taught them to enjoy the greater and no more exacting game; the perfect companion who never wasted a word in idle chatter, was never put out, laughed loudest in disaster, was humble to a fault, and staunch unto death. As a school boy his physique was magnificent, but as he was truly formidable in action, none was more gentle off the field or where duty permitted relaxation, and his great gift of leadership was crowned by the respect he accorded without abating any of his demands upon him, to the smallest, weakest member of the house or school. We do not know the manner of his passing but at least we know that death found him unmoved, unhurried, undismayed, with the game for which he had played, as he had always played soundly and honourably won.

Marshall has no known grave. He is commemorated on the Plymouth Naval memorial, panel 95, column 3. He is also commemorated at Giggleswick and at his old Oxford College.

France

Emile Doussau
One test
Died 28 April 1940, aged 31
Prop

Died in a tragic car accident returning from a rugby match

Emile Doussau was born on 7 March 1909 at Charmant in south-west France. A countryman and farmer by profession. He was serving in the army during 1940 at the time of his tragic death.

Emile only played in one test, against Romania on 15 May 1938, at the Dinamo Stadion, Bucharest, in the Fédération Internationale de rugby Amateur (FIRA) tournament which had begun in 1934 outside the authority of the International rugby Football Board. France were 0-11 up at half time but Romania fought back hard in the second half. The final score being 8-11 to France, Jean Blond, Robert Caunegre and Raymond le Goff getting the tries and Joseph Desclaux kicking a conversion. France went on to beat Nazi German on 28 May 1938 and win the tournament (Doussau failed to play in the match against Germany).

Emile died on 28 April 1940 in a car accident at Charmant (near Angoulème) while returning from a rugby match.

Private François Meret
France
One test
Died 10 June 1940
Aged 26
Prop

Played in France's first match after their expulsion in 1931

François Meret was born on 8 June 1914 at Pontacq (between Pau and Lourdes), France. He worked most of his early life in a shoe factory, marrying a local girl twelve days before he was called up and marched off to war.

He played one international game for France against the British Army on 25 February 1940 at the Parc des Princes. In a very one-sided affair the British Army crushed France by three points to thirty-six, Pierre Thiers scoring the only French points with a penalty. It was the first representative match between France and the home nations since their expulsion from the Five Nations in 1931. The home nations had formally readmitted France in 1939, but the decision was made in July, long after that season's tournament concluded, and in the knowledge that war would very likely intervene.

Meret was killed in action on 10 June 1940 in north-eastern France.

The Parc des Princes, pictured in 1932.

**Sergeant Georges 'Géo' André
Seven tests
French Free Corps
Died 4 May 1943, aged 53
Wing**

France's greatest sporting hero

Georges Yvan André, known as Géo, was born on 13 August 1889 in Paris. He was educated at the École Supérieure d'Électricité and the École Supérieure de l'Aeronautique. An outstanding athlete he was the French champion in the 400 metres, the 110 and 400 metres hurdles, the standing high jump and the high jump. He also held national records in many of these events. He competed as a track and field athlete in the Olympic Games in 1908, 1912, 1920 and 1924. He took part in the long jump, the high jump, the standing high jump, the hurdles and the 400 metres sprint, as well as competing in the pentathlon and decathlon. He won the silver medal in the high jump in 1908 and a bronze in the 4 X 400 metres relay in 1920. During the 1924 Games he took the Olympic Oath on behalf of all athletes and had the honour of being the flag bearer for France at the opening ceremony.

As well as being a fine athlete he was also a fine rugby player, representing Racing Club de France and playing on the wing. His speed and strength were quickly recognized; one commentator said of him, 'As a wing he ran with an unusual action, a legacy of his expertise as a hurdler, and was a difficult opponent to halt.'

He was soon selected to play for the French XV and represented them on seven consecutive occasions between 1913 and '14. He made his debut against South Africa on 11 January 1913 at the Stade Sainte Germaine in Bordeaux. The French were overwhelmed and went down by five points to thirty-eight. Maurice Bruneau got France's only try and André managed to kick the conversion, his first international points.

His next appearance was against England at Twickenham during the Five Nations on 25 January 1913. This time they lost by twenty points to zero. Wales were next on 27 February at the Parc des Princes. The French put up a good fight and were only just defeated by eight points to eleven. André grounded his first try, Pierre Failliot grounding a second. Philippe Struxiano kicked a conversion.

France

The final match of the Five Nations series was played on 24 March 1913 at the Mardyke, Cork. The Irish ran riot defeating France by twenty-four points to zero.

Despite the previous season's whitewash André was chosen to play for France again in 1914. The season commenced against Ireland on 1 January 1914 at the Parc des Princes. This time it was a different match to the previous seasons. France were 3-0 up at half time and although they finally went down by six points to eight it was a near run thing and France played well. André got another try down, Robert Lacoste getting a second. In the end Ireland kicked one of their conversions and France missed both of theirs. It decided the game.

Their next game was against Wales at St Helen's, Swansea. Unfortunately their success against Ireland wasn't replicated against Wales and they went down by thirty-one points to zero.

André's final international match was against England at the Stade Olympique on 13 April 1914. France played well and, although defeated thirteen points to thirty-nine, the outcome did not reflect the French effort. André managed another try on his final appearance, together with Marcel-Frédéric Lubin-Lebrère. Lucien Besset kicked two conversions.

The outbreak of war in 1914 put an end to his career, as with hundreds of others.

A physical training instructor, he had joined the 103ème Régiment d'Infanterie on 12 October 1910, and was mobilized on 2 August 1914. He was promoted to corporal on 1 September, then to sergeant on 2 September. He was seriously wounded and captured shortly afterwards. Spending several years in captivity he made five attempts to escape, being recaptured each time. On the sixth occasion he made it, returning to France and training as a fighter pilot before joining the Stork Squadron in November 1917. He was awarded the Military Medal and was wounded by a bullet through the ankle during a dog-fight. He was demobilized after the war aged 30. His wounds however had taken their toll and it was some time before he could resume his sporting career. As mentioned previously he competed in both the 1920 and 1924 Olympics.

After completing his sporting career he became a journalist writing for the *Mirror Sport* and *The Excelsior*. He also wrote several books on sports.

Keen to do his bit during the Second World War, but at 53 too old to be a pilot, he joined the French Free Corps in Africa in 1942. André was killed in action at Mateur, Bizerte, during the advance on Tunis on 4 May 1943. There is some evidence that he might have been captured and shot by the SS as a member of the Resistance (I'm still researching this).

Final Scrum

The commemorative plaque in Paris reads as follows: 'Here lived Geo Andre, hero of the fight for liberty, who died for France. Killed at the head of his company, in Tunis, May 1943'.

He was a great loss to French sport and was mourned across the nation. Many sporting stadiums in France are named after this sporting giant and French hero, including one in Paris, and a commemorative plaque in his honour has been unveiled at 9 Rue Marguerin, Paris, his former home.

André had married and had two children. His son Jacques (1919-88) competed in the 1948 Olympics as a hurdler. He was also a sixteen-kill ace during the Second World War. His father would have been very proud.

France

Henri Levée
One test
Civilian
Died 26 March 1943, aged 58
Centre

A victim of the Holocaust

Henri Levée was born on 17 March 1885 in Paris. He worked as an industrial manager and played his club rugby for the Racing Club de France. He played in one test for France against the New Zealand All Blacks while they were on their European tour. The match was played on 1 January 1906 at the Parc des Princes. It was very much a one-sided affair with New Zealand winning the game by eight points to thirty-eight (New Zealand grounding ten tries), Noel Cessieux and Georges Jerome getting two down for France, Augustin Pujol kicking a conversion.

Levée served throughout the First World War, managed to survive, and continued with his civilian job on his return.

He was rounded up as a Jew shortly after the German invasion of France in 1940 and deported to the German concentration camp at Sachsenhausen, an evil place where Levée was to suffer hunger and cruelty at the hands of his SS guards. Some 30,000 inmates died at this camp, including Levée – the exact cause of his death is unknown.

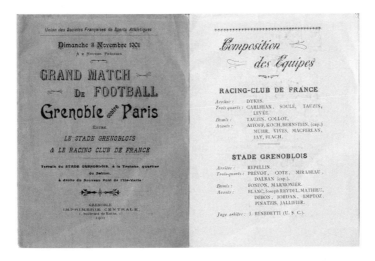

Roger Claudel
France
Two tests
Died 8 December 1944, aged 33
Flanker

Defeated Germany twice

Roger Claudel was born on 10 April 1911 at Chartres. He was a salesman by trade. He played his club rugby for Lyon Olympique Universitaire who were French champions in the 1931-2 season, defeating Narbonne at the Parc des Sports, Bordeaux, 9-3 (LOU had lost in the championship the previous year, defeated by Toulon 6-3).

Claudel made two test appearances, both against Germany. The first took place on 17 April 1932 at Frankfurt. In front of a crowd of 4,000, France ran amok defeating Germany by twenty points to four. Marcel Baillette, Eugène Chaud, Jean Coderc and René Finat (x2) scored tries, Chaud also kicked a conversion and Max Rousie kicked a penalty.

The Lyon Olympique Universitaire team. Roger Claudel is believed to be in this photograph, although it is unclear which of the men is him.

Claudel had to wait two years for his next appearance, again against Germany. The match was played in Hanover on 25 March 1934. France won the game but only just, Germany finally going down by nine points to thirteen, Joseph Desclaux, Andre Duluc and Pierre Cussac scoring a try each. Chaud and Desclaux kicked a conversion each. It was Claudel's final international appearance.

He died on 8 December 1944 at Rammers in the area of Haut-Rhin in Alsace near Colmar.

Allan Muhr
Three tests
Red Cross (Ambulance Driver)
Died 29 December 1944, aged 62
Lock

Played in France's first international rugby match

Allan Henry Muhr was born in Philadelphia on 23 January 1882. His family, who were Jewish, moved to France during the early part of the twentieth century. Muhr was educated at the prestigious Lycée Janson, reading French. Learning the French language quickly helped him secure his position with the rugby team, Racing Club. He played second line or prop, earning, because of his somewhat Native American appearance, the nickname 'The Sioux'. While playing rugby, which was the greatest passion of his life, he also worked as a sporting journalist. He had a considerable private income and one commentator said of him in 1907, 'He amazes us because he is not the slave of any bureau chief or other boss or editor, still less of the rulers of the USFSA [the French sporting authorities of the time]. He does what he pleases when he pleases.'

Allan's passion for the game got him selected for France's very first test match, against the New Zealand All Blacks on 1 January 1906. The match was played at the Parc des Princes in front of a crowd of 3,000. France went down heavily by eight points to thirty-eight, Noël Cessieux and Georges Jérome getting the ball down for France.

He next turned out against England, at the Parc des Princes on 22 March 1906. It was the first time the two sides had ever met. Once again it was a crushing defeat, by thirty-five points to eight, however Muhr did manage to get his first international points by grounding one of France's two tries, crossing after brilliant work by Stade Français centre Pierre Maclos. Émile Lesieur grounded the second.

Muhr's final international was against England again, this time at the Athletic Ground, Richmond, on 5 January 1907. Although the match was drawing thirteen points each at half time, thanks to Muhr's efforts in getting the ball down in the corner the second half was a different matter. The Harlequins wing, Daniel Lambert, crossed the line five times, helping England to a forty-one points to thirteen victory. Marcel Communeau scored a second try for France while Paul Maclos kicked two conversions and a penalty. Muhr picked up a serious knee injury in 1907, which put an end to his international career. However Muhr wasn't one for letting things go. He became chair of the French selectors, his first match in charge being the historic victory over Scotland.

Also a fine tennis player he reached the final of the Etretat tournament in 1909 and captained the French Davis Cup team in 1912.

During the First World War, Muhr served first as an ambulance driver, and then helped form the Lafayette Escadrille, a squadron of American fliers fighting for the French, including the first black pilot Eugene Bullard, who had previously been fighting with a French infantry regiment despite being an American citizen.

After the war Muhr helped establish the French Rugby Federation in 1919, serving as its president and played a major part in bringing the 1924 Olympics to France.

At the beginning of the Second World War, Muhr served once again as a volunteer ambulance driver, with the Red Cross. After the fall of France in 1940 Muhr, with several other Americans, hid in Sayat in the Auvergne. From there they gave what assistance they could to the French Resistance. However on 21 November Muhr and two of his friends were betrayed and arrested by the SS. He was taken to a camp at Compiègne where he was brutally interrogated and they discovered he was Jewish. The following May he was deported to Germany. The gallant Muhr was starved to death in a concentration camp at Neuengamme near Hamburg, dying on the 29 December 1944.

He was later awarded a posthumous Légion d'Honneur for his sporting and heroic services to France.

Captain Étienne Piquiral
France
Nineteen tests
248th Regiment of heavy artillery
13th March 1945, aged 43
Back row

Took the silver medal for rugby in the 1924 Olympics

Étienne Piquiral was born on 15 June 1901 in Perpignan, Pyrénées-Orientales. He was the third child of Julien Louis Piquiral and Rosalie Come. His father, who worked for the telegraph, was transferred to Périgeux in the Dordogne and Piquiral was educated at the local city high school followed by the École Polytechnique in 1921 for whom he played rugby.

Deciding on a career in the army he took a commission as a second lieutenant in the artillery, attending the School of Artillery and Engineering at Fontainebleau. He completed his studies in September 1924. Piquiral played his club rugby for CA Périgourdin, Racing Club de France, and later for the Lyon football (rugby) club. He also played for the French Army.

Piquiral made nineteen test appearances for France between 1924 and 1928. He made his debut against Scotland on 1 January 1924 at the Stade Pershing. Against most people's expectations, France won the game by twelve points to ten, with Piquiral grounding his first try and gaining his first points for France, Henri Galau, Adolphe Jauréguy and Pierre Moureu grounding one more try each. Against Ireland a few weeks later, on 26 January at Lansdowne Road, they lost, but only by six points to three in a hard-fought match. Against England on 23 February at Twickenham, France went down again by nineteen points to seven, Jacques Ballarin getting a try and André Béhotéguy dropping a goal.

France's final match of the 1924 Five Nations was against Wales on 27 March at the Stade Olympique. France played well, only going down by six points to ten, Béhotéguy and Lubin-Lebrère getting a try each. France ended the season joint fourth with Wales.

Piquiral was next selected to play rugby for France during the 1924 Olympics in Paris, officially known as the Games of the VIII Olympiad (France had previously held the Games in 1900). Only three sides took part: France, Romania and the USA. France's first game was against Romania on 4 May 1924 at the Stade Olympique, Colombes, Paris (all the matches were played at the

Colombes). France ran amok, defeating Romania by sixty-one points to three, grounding no fewer than thirteen tries. Their next match was against the USA in the Olympic final. France's star player Adolphe Jauréguy was knocked cold and injured in the first few minutes of the game and had to be taken off the field. After that, the largely French crowd booed and hissed the American team, which had a reputation for rough play. Later, bottles and rocks were thrown at them and fights started in the stands. The US reserve Gideon Nelson was knocked unconscious after being hit in the face by a walking stick. The American team

finally came out victors by three points to seventeen, taking the Olympic gold medal and leaving France with the silver. Henri Galau got the only try and points for France. At the end of the match the French fans invaded the pitch and it was only down to the bravery of the French team and police that the Americans weren't attacked. During the medal ceremony the American national anthem was drowned out by the boos of the crowd.

Piquiral only played once during the 1925 Five Nations against England, on 13 April at the Stade Olympique. It was a hard-fought match with France getting three tries to England's two, however William Luddington managed to kick two conversions and a goal from the mark, which made the difference, England winning by the narrow margin of eleven points to thirteen. France came back strongly in the second half but did not quite make it. France ended the Five Nations last.

Piquiral was selected for the Five Nations in 1926 and played in all four matches. It was to be a poor season, with France losing all their matches. Against Scotland, 6-20, Piquiral managing to get a try down. Against Ireland, 11-0, against England, 11-0 and finally against Wales, 5-7.

France played one further match in 1926 against the visiting New Zealand Maoris. The match took place on 26 December at the Stade Olympique, France going down to the visitors by three points to twelve.

Selected for the Five Nations once again in 1927, they lost their first three games: against Ireland 3-8, against Scotland 23-6, Piquiral getting one of two tries. After losing to Wales twenty-five points to seven, France faced England.

The match was played on 2 April at the Stade Olympique and much to everyone's surprise France took the match by three points to zero, Edmond Vellat getting the ball down for France. France finished joint fourth with Wales.

Piquiral next took on the Germans during their tour of France. The first match took place on 17 April 1927 at the Stade Olympique, France trouncing Germany thirty points to five. He next played against Germany on 15 May, this time in Frankfurt. France were the favourites but Germany took the match by one point – seventeen points to sixteen. Piquiral made his final appearance for France on 25 February 1928 against England at Twickenham. England played the better rugby and defeated France by eighteen points to eight.

During the Second World War Piquiral was mobilized and fought against Germany with the 248th Regiment of heavy artillery. His position was overrun and he was captured by the Germans on 23 June 1940 at Toul (Meurthe-et-Moselle). He was sent to Oflag X-B in Nienburg, Germany where he was imprisoned for over four years. He became ill and died there on 13 March 1945.

Sergeant Georges Vaills
France
Two tests
Died 30 March 1945
Hooker

Had a stadium named after him

Georges Vaills was born on 6 December 1903 at Palau del Vidre (near Perpignan). He worked for Perpignan city gardens and sport grounds. He played his club rugby for Racing Club Palauenc founded in 1920 (now Palau XIII Broncos) in the Palau-del-Vidre.

He made two international appearances, the first on 22 January 1928 against Australia at the Stade Olympique. France was 3-11 down at half time, fought back hard, but still lost 8-11. Raoul Bonamy and André Camel scored tries and André Béhotéguy kicked a conversion. His second international took place against Germany on 28 April 1929 again at the Stade Olympique. This time France took the honours by twenty-four points to zero. Marcel Baillette and Marcel Soler scored two tries each, and André Duche and Jules Hauc one each.

Serving with the army, Vaills was captured and taken prisoner during the early part of the Second World War. He remained incarcerated in Germany for the duration, dying as a prisoner on 30 March 1945.

The Stade Georges Vaills in Palau-del-Vidre where Vaills had made so many appearances was named in his memory.

Ireland

Commander Charles Hallaran
Albert Medal
Ireland
Fifteen tests
Royal Navy, HMS *Springbank*
Died 21 March 1941, aged 43
Lock

'A priceless man'
Gave his life to save a junior sailor

Charles Francis George Thomas Hallaran was born on 10 June 1897 in Ceylon. He was the son of Colonel William Hallaran of the Indian Army and educated at Eastman's Royal Naval Academy College followed by the Royal Naval College Dartmouth. He played in the first XV at Dartmouth where his talent for the game was quickly recognized.

He was commissioned as a midshipman on 2 August 1914 and served on the Iron Duke-class battleship HMS *Benbow* from 1914, taking part in the Battle of Jutland in 1916. In the same year he was transferred to the Azalea-class sloop HMS *Zinnia* and became involved in submarine hunting being awarded an MiD (*London Gazette* 10 August 1917) for his services against enemy submarines. He was promoted sub-lieutenant in 1917 and served on HMS *Resolution* for the remainder of the war, seeing no further action. He was promoted to lieutenant in 1918.

His father Colonel William Hallaran played once for Ireland against Wales on 12 April 1884. Oddly, he played the match under the pseudonym R.O.N. Hall – his father was the archdeacon of Ardfelt and formerly canon of St. Mary's, Limerick, and apparently wouldn't have approved. Serving with the Royal Army Medical Corps, Colonel William became a surgeon and died in Jabalpur, India, on 23 January 1917 while director of medical services. His name is on the Sir Patrick Dun's Hospital Great War Memorial, Dublin.

Charles continued with his rugby playing for the Royal Navy as well appearing five times for the Barbarians between 1920 and 1923. He played against Penarth, Swansea, Neath, and the Leicester Tigers twice. He also turned out for Surrey RFC. Hallaran made fifteen international appearances for Ireland between 1921 and '26.

He made his debut in the Five Nations against England at Twickenham on 12 February 1921. Seven players made their debut that day which might go someway to explaining their 15-0 defeat. He next appeared against Scotland on 26 February at Lansdowne Road, Dublin, being defeated by the narrow score of 9-8. Against Wales on 12 March at the Balmoral Showgrounds, Belfast, Ireland went down again, this time 0-6. It was Hallaran's final game of the 1921 season (he didn't play in the final match of the season against France on 9 April; Ireland lost the match twenty points to ten). Ireland finished last getting the wooden spoon having made only two points to show for their efforts.

Keeping faith with Hallaran, he was selected to play once again during the 1922 Five Nations. The season kicked off against England on 11 February at Lansdowne Road, Ireland going down by three points to twelve. Scotland were next at Inverleith. Ireland went down again, this time by six points to three, although they had been three up at half time. Against Wales at St Helen's, Swansea, on 11 March, Ireland were defeated again, this time by eleven points to five (as with the season before Hallaran didn't play against France which was unfortunate as Ireland beat them by eight points to three).

Hallaran was only selected for two matches during the 1923 season. The first against England at Welford Road, Leicester, on 10 February, England taking the match by fifteen points to five. He next appeared against France at the Stade Olympique, Paris, on 14 April. Alas France got the better of them winning the game by fourteen points to eight (Hallaran failed to play in the 3-13 defeat against Scotland on 24 February and the 5-4 victory against Wales on 10 March).

Keeping faith with Hallaran for the 1924 season, he played in all four matches. At last he played in a winning side as Ireland defeated France on 26 January at Lansdowne Road six points to zero. Against England at Ravenhill, Belfast, on 9 February it was a different matter as Ireland was defeated by three points to fourteen. They were then defeated against Scotland on 23 February at Inverleith, thirteen points to eight. In the match against Wales at the National Stadium, Wales, on 8 March 1924, which Wales were favourites to win, Ireland pulled of a surprise victory by ten points to thirteen.

He only played in one match during the 1925 season, against France on 1 January at the Stade Olympique, Ireland taking the match by three points to nine.

The 1926 season was to be his last and he was selected twice, firstly against France on 26 January at Ravenhill, Belfast, Ireland taking the match by eleven points to zero. He played his final game for Ireland against the old enemy England at Lansdowne Road on 13 February. In a hard-fought contest Ireland defeated England by nineteen points to fifteen, despite England being up by ten points to six at half time. Ireland shared the championship with Scotland with six points each (Ireland also defeated Scotland by zero points to three and lost to Wales by eleven points to eight).

Charles married twice, firstly to Annita Linsay Sinclair in February 1924 and secondly to Elizabeth Joyce Philpott in 1934.

He was put onto the retired list in 1934 at his own request. By 1939 however he was back serving with the Navy with the rank of commander (retired). He was given command of the anti-aircraft ship HMS *Springbank*. It was while in command of this vessel that the brave Albert Hallaran was to lose his life. *The Times* later described what happened:

The Times, 10 September 1941
NAVAL AWARDS
COMMANDER'S LIFE FOR A STOKER
JUMP INTO ROUGH SEA

ALBERT MEDAL (POSTHUMOUS)
Cdr. Albert Francis George Thomas HALLARAN, R.N.

On a very dark night a motor-boat came alongside Cdr. Hallaran's ship to take off the pilot. A swell made this boat roll and pitch heavily, and a stoker was thrown overboard between it and the ship's side. He was seen to be in difficulties, and was in danger of being crushed as the swell kept heaving the boat against the ship. Cdr. Hallaran climbed into the boat, jumped into the sea, and swam round to help him. He got the stoker back to the boat, but as he did so was thrown against it. His skull was fractured and he was drowned before he could be got back on board.

HMS *Springbank*.

For his brave actions that night Hallaran was awarded the Albert Medal posthumously. A fellow officer later wrote a warm tribute to him which was published in *The Times* on 4 September 1941:

> *I crave your indulgence that I may write a word in personal sorrow at the quick and untimely death that claimed my brother officer, Charles Hallaran – I had only known him a few months – short, as many of his friendships go – but in that time I, and all of us had come to rest upon him as the pillar of his ship's existence. He had a sure sense of affairs and was an utterly loyal senior – a priceless man. In duty inflexible, in pleasure he was warm, and the widespread company of those who mourn him will testify to the gaiety and sunshine of his spirit. His tantrums were great – as tremendous as himself. He had a mighty joy in a row, whether he was right or wrong. What did it matter! all was soon blown over, and once more that slow and attractive smile would take the sting from any words of his. We his messmates miss him. We are leaderless. No greater tribute can we give than to say how hollowly we feel an absence where once, so lately, dwelt such a massive presence.*

He is commemorated in the Belfast City Cemetery, Glenalina Extension, section D, grave 125.

A group photograph of the 1924 Irish national team. Hallaran can be seen seated on the right.

Wing Commander Patric (Paddy) Coote
Ireland
One test
211 Squadron Royal Air Force
Died 13 April 1941, aged 31
Centre

Beat Douglas Bader to the Sword of Honour

Patric Bernard Coote, better known as Paddy, was born on 7 January 1910 at Eton, near Windsor. He was one of five sons of Commander Bernard Trotter Coote, RN, OBE and Grace (née Robinson). He was educated, like his four brothers Denis, Henry, Roderic and Philip, at Woking County Grammar School where, like his four brothers, he excelled at sports. He was quick on his feet, winning the 100, 220 and 440 metres, as well as the hurdles, long jump, high jump, and throwing the cricket ball. He was also a decent bat.

On leaving school he joined the RAF and in 1926, having passed the boy mechanic exams in 1923, became an aircraft apprentice stationed at RAF Halton. A bright boy, in 1928 he was awarded the Sir Charles Wakefield Scholarship of £75 for an apprenticeship/cadetship at the RAF College Cranwell. In July 1930 he was awarded the Sword of Honour for being the most outstanding student at Cranwell, beating the famous Douglas Bader into second place. He was also awarded the Air Ministry prize for aeronautical engineering, achieving some of the highest marks ever.

Despite his academic record he didn't forget his sports, which he clearly loved. He excelled at putting the weight, played hockey for Cranwell, and won the RAF squash championship in 1931, coming second the following year despite having picked up a rugby injury. He also boxed and was a keen athlete. In 1931 he was a member of the RAF four-man bobsleigh team that took part in the Gold Cup in St Moritz together with Pilot Officer Dennis Field (steersman), Pilot Officer Ralph Wallace and Pilot Officer Jack Newcomb (brakeman). (Newcomb fell ill and died of peritonitis shortly after the games on 26 Feb 1931.) They took the bronze, Germany taking the gold and Switzerland the silver.

Playing rugby for the RAF against the Royal Navy in 1931, he played together with his old friend and rival Douglas Bader (Bader didn't lose his legs until December of that year). In October he played for London against South Africa at Twickenham. London were out-matched and lost by a large margin:

Coote can be seen here, seated third from the right in 1931. The RAF Ace and hero Douglas Bader is seated on the far right.

30-3. In 1933 he played for the East Midlands against Warwickshire. Between 1931 and '33 he played twenty-seven times for Leicester and his continual good form got him noticed by the Irish selectors. He turned out against Scotland on 1 April 1933 at Lansdowne Road, Dublin. In a hard-fought match Scotland finally edged it by six points to eight. It was to be Patric's only international appearance. In December 1933 while playing for Leicester away to Swansea he suffered a heavy tackle and sustained a serious neck injury and concussion. The injury was so bad he was hospitalized for several months at the RAF hospital Uxbridge. The injury alas put an end to his rugby career.

In September 1931 he trained as a flying instructor, returning to Cranwell as an instructor. In 1933 he was posted to the Central Flying School at Upavon and the following year became adjutant with a bomb squadron.

He married in 1935 Muriel Elsmie and they had two daughters, Anne and Brigid. Promoted to flight lieutenant in 1936 he was posted to the Middle East as an instructor, later being transferred to the British Military Mission in Egypt. He was later promoted to squadron leader and then in December 1940 wing commander, being posted to 211 Squadron in Paramythia in Greece. On 28 February 1941 while flying a Gloster Gladiator, Paddy got his one and only kill of the war shooting down an Italian Fiat CR42a near the Tepelene coast in southern Albania.

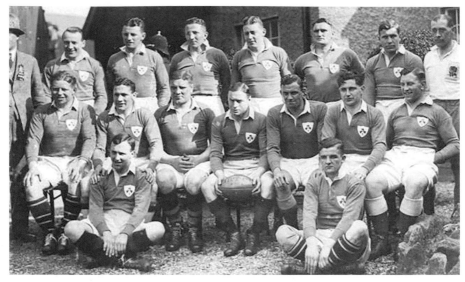

Coote can be seen standing, second from the right as part of the 1933 Irish team.

On 13 April 1941 Patric decided to fly as an observer on one of six Bristol Blenheims, L4819, during a raid on Florina in the Monastir. The formation was led by Squadron Leader Irvine, the commanding officer, a 27-year-old Old Etonian. As the squadron approached Lake Prespa they were spotted and attacked by three Messerschmitt Bf108s of 6/JG27 based at Gazala in Libya. In only a few minutes all six Blenheims were shot down. Patric's plane was shot down by the twenty-nine-kill German ace Unteroffizier Fritz Gromotka (his second kill) and crashed near the village of Trigonon. There were no survivors. Only two members of the squadron survived: Flight Lieutenant A.C. Godfrey and Flight Sergeant A.G. James. Godfrey later recalled,

> We were ordered to dive. Next thing the cockpit was a mass of flames. As they blazed up in my face I tore the hatch back and jumped. I noticed that there were three aircraft in the air – all in flames. My crew was dead.

The other members of Patric's crew were Flying Officer Richard V. Herbert and Flight Sergeant William Young. Herbert, aged 21, managed to bail out but the aircraft was too low and he did not survive (both his brothers were also killed during the war).

Patric is buried in Phaleron War Cemetery, near Athens (grave 4.C.19). He is also remembered on the Woking County Grammar School roll of honour in Christ Church, Woking and on Woodham war memorial.

Ireland

Major Edward (Ted) Hunt
Ireland
Five tests
Royal Artillery
1 Hong Kong Regiment
Died 20 December 1941, aged 33
Centre

Thus passes another magnificent rugby player

Edward William Francis de Vere Hunt was born on 12 December 1908 in Dorset. He was the son of John Theodore de Vere Hunt and Ada Mary. He was educated at the Dragon School between 1919 and 1922 where he picked up the nickname Bunch. An outstanding athlete he was in the first XV, the hockey XI, the football XI the cricket XI. He also won the 100 yards, the high jump, hurdles and boxing. He carried off the Hockey Cup, the Boxing Cup, a School Bat, and the Denis O'Sullivan Cup for the best all-round athlete. He was also a fine academic. Moving up to Rugby School he became head of house and ran, jumped and boxed for the school as well as getting his colours for cricket, rugby and hockey. Leaving Rugby in 1927 and deciding on a career in the army he went up to the Royal Military Academy, Woolwich. He once again displayed his fine athleticism winning his cricket, rugby and boxing colours. He passed out in 1929 being commissioned into the Royal Artillery being based at Aldershot until 1936. It was during these years that Hunt was to reach his rugby peak. He played for the Army, Rosslyn Park, Hampshire, Major Stanley's XV, The Barbarians and Oxfordshire. The England and Gloucester legend D.R. Gent said of him,

> His personality and his delightful demeanour on the rugby field, whatever the match and whether he was playing for Rosslyn Park, the Army, or Ireland, always fascinated me. That he was a beautiful player of this grand man's game was, in a way, incidental. It was his good temper, his desire to be all over the place at once, his pluck, his lovely flair for taking chances, his attractive physical figure surmounted by that mop of fair hair – these are a few of the features that kept me watching him all the time.

Bunch went on to win five caps for Ireland between 1930 and 1933. He made his debut against France in the Five Nations at Ravenhill, Belfast, on 25 January 1930. It wasn't a great start as Ireland went down by five points to zero. Missing

95

Hunt can be seen here on the back row, third from the left in 1933.

the 1931 season, he was selected again in 1932, playing against England on 13 February at Lansdowne Road. Once again Hunt was to be on the losing side as Ireland went down by eight points to eleven – a near run thing. Two weeks later, on 27 February, he was selected to play against Scotland at Murrayfield. This time it was Ireland that took the honours, winning the game by eight points to twenty. Hunt scored one of the four tries. It was the first and last time he scored for his country. Ireland continued with their winning ways against Wales on 12 March 1932 at the National Stadium, Cardiff, beating them by ten points to twelve and sharing the championship with England and Wales. Hunt made his final international appearance against England on 11 February 1933 at Twickenham. England was the better team and took the match by seventeen points to three.

A good description of Hunt appears in the book *Barbarian Football Club 1890-1955* by Andrew Wemyss:

A UNIQUE IRISHMAN

E.W.F. de Vere Hunt, the Irish full-back and centre three-quarter, was just one of the host of outstanding players who have added something out of the ordinary to my rambling story.

That he won a tense game against Newport by dropping a goal in the last minute is worth mention though not more so than other match winning feats I have recalled. 'Ted' Hunt, however, developed into one of the many personalities who added gaiety to Barbarian occasions both off and on the field and I will never forget how a frantic run he made at Cardiff gave the crowd at the Arms Park surely the biggest laugh they had ever had. It was so comical and altogether extraordinary that it reduced nearly all the players, friend and foe alike, to a state of laughing immobility.

Hunt was on his first tour and playing full-back when he won the match at Rodney Parade in 1929. I can see it now, a tall athletic figure with the fresh complexion of an unshaven boy, his flaxen hair parted in the middle and wearing Rosslyn Park stockings. He had been competent in everything he did, but hardly looked like making a memorable contribution to the game. Newport, with only minutes to play, were leading by a penalty goal kicked by their international full-back, Bill Everson. We, however, were attacking strongly in an endeavour to save the game when, to the consternation of the home supporters, for they seldom see such things, a wild clearing kick went upfield towards Hunt, who was standing almost on the centre spot. Ted gathered that rather round pumpkin of a ball and, with the calm assurance of a Bancroft, to everyone's amazement he sent it sailing between the posts with a beautiful drop kick. That meant four points in those days and an altogether unexpected win for us.

Hughie and I walked round to the station together for the journey back to London and all the way we hooted with laughter as we discussed our win and how Ted had seemed the most unlikely player in the wide world, as he stood on the field, even to have a go let alone score from 50 yards range.

As a prelude to the Cardiff incident I have to explain that when playing for Ireland there a few weeks earlier in the 1932 international which Ireland had won 12-10, Hunt had caused Wales a lot of trouble, one being the manner in which he got out of seemingly safe tackles.

Against Cardiff we were playing towards the Taff end and pressing in the vicinity of the '25' flag on the new stand side near the players' entrance. From a maul Cardiff got the ball. It went back to Harry Bowcott at stand-off and instead of clearing to touch down the stand side he kicked away across towards our '25' on the opposite side. I was running the line in front of the old stand and had a perfect close-up of all that happened.

The ball did not reach touch by a bit. It kept rolling and bumping, and with R.W. Langrish as full-back guarding the line on the other side, Ted Hunt came after it. As he ran back after it, however, he could not gather it. He kept knocking it out of his reach as Little Tich used to do with his elongated boots when he was trying to pick up his silk hat in his well-known comic stage act.

By this time four Cardiff forwards, with a glint in their eyes which showed they were not going to allow Hunt to repeat his 'international' nonsense, were closing *for the kill. Ted at last picked up the ball, but no sooner was it in his hands when the human avalanche arrived.*

Crash, bang, wallop, thud, and as I looked to see if no help was coming Ted suddenly jumped out of the welter of arms and legs and raced away straight across our '25' line. Langrish, who had got back to the vicinity of the posts, like everyone else was bewildered and I thought to myself, 'Good heavens, he'll be away out the other side of the ground and up Westgate Street if nobody stops him.'

However, when he was nearly at the other side Ted apparently took a look at his compass, suddenly changed direction and went tearing up the other side of the pitch. After whistling past about the only two Cardiff players capable of moving, Hunt found Ben Tod racing alongside, although he, too, was bursting with laughter. Then, as if to say 'That's been great fun, Ben, you have a go now,' Hunt gave the ball to Tod who scorched the remaining 30 yards or so to score an astonishing try which Brian Black converted.

My other yarn about Hunt is all-Irish, he and Paddy Coote as opponents at centre taking part in the wildly exciting race which ended not with a try but a great saving tackle in the Leicester match of 1931.

Play was close to the Tigers' line and our full-back, Leslie Bedford, joined in an attack which broke down. In a flash Paddy Coote gathered the loose ball and set off for the pavilion end with no-one to beat.

When Hunt took up the chase he was more than a good five yards behind and as Coote crossed the centre line it seemed he was bound to score. Running like a man possessed, however, the Baa-Baa skipper gradually narrowed the gap, and as he closed the roar of the crowd was tremendous. Fifteen yards to go, then ten and still Hunt was just out of distance. But when it looked hopeless he hurled himself through the air and made a brilliant tackle which felled Coote to the ground just inches short of the line.

Hunt married Nancy Rudkin on 5 July 1934 at St Nicholas Church, Compton, Guildford.

In 1937 he was sent to Egypt where he kept up his athletic endeavours becoming a member of the Royal Horse Artillery Polo Team winning the Inter-Regimental Cup in Cairo. In 1938 he was sent to Palestine and promoted to captain. He was then forced to leave his beloved Royal Horse Artillery and travel to Hong Kong to assist with coastal defences. Promoted to major he was still in Hong Kong when war broke out. He formed and commanded a new Beach Battery which he did in quick time. Ordered to return to England these orders were rescinded at the last minute and he took up command of the 1st Mountain Battery. He was still in command of them when the Japanese army attacked. Forced to withdraw on 13 December 1941 he took over command of the Eastern Group Royal Artillery. He led a successful counter-attack before returning to his battle HQ. However while he was there the Japanese launched their own counter-attack and took the position. Returning quickly to his battery he found it under heavy and continual shell fire. He was seriously wounded by one of these shells but refused to be evacuated and remained at his post helping to fire his gun. When his men tried to get him to retire he refused, repeating the words, 'Plenty of time, plenty of time for me.' He got all his wounded soldiers away before going out to search for anymore who might have been left out in the open. He found several and managed to get them evacuated. Finally on 20 December he managed to get to hospital and have some treatment. It was while he was returning from the hospital at the Wong Nai Chang Gap he disappeared. It was some time before his death was confirmed. His desperate wife even advertised in *The Times* on 14 March 1942, requesting information on his whereabouts. His death was finally confirmed in June 1944. *The Sunday Times* contained the following obituary:

It has now been officially reported that Major E. W. F. de Vere Hunt, R.A., was killed during the fighting at Hong-Kong in December 1941. We heard at the time how superbly he had led his men, and the worst was feared. Thus passes another magnificent rugby player, for between 1929 and 1933 there was nobody more attractive to watch in every country than this tall, fair-haired, care-free Irishman...

The Times said of him,

De Vere Hunt was not the man to wait until the game came his way; he went to look for work. The result was that you saw his active figure, dominated by his exceptionally fair hair, all over the field, to the great discomfiture of his opponents, and often even of his colleagues! I saw him in that great game at Cardiff in 1932, when Wales were fully expected to beat Ireland and so win the much-coveted Triple Crown. But glorious football by Hunt, W. McC. Ross, Paul Murray, George Beamish, and Eugene Davy enabled Ireland to win by four tries to a dropped goal and two tries. Grand games I call to mind, too, that he played for the Barbarians at Leicester, and as centre to A. L. Novis for the Army. Hunt was 'the Happy Warrior,' and the rugby world mourns another ornament to the game.

He is commemorated on the Sai Wan Memorial, Hong Kong.

Lieutenant Colonel John Minch
Ireland
Five tests
Royal Army Medical Corps
Died 8 November 1942, aged 52
Centre

Paddy was one of the real characters of the Corps and the stories of his doings
and sayings were many and varied

John Berchmans Minch, known as Paddy, was born on 29 July 1890 at Athy, Co Kildare. He was the second son of Matthew Joseph Minch of Rockfield House, Athy, MP for South Kildare and owner of Minch Malt, the largest maltsters in Ireland. He was educated at Clongowes Wood College and University College Dublin, graduating MBBCh in 1914. He was also a BA in obstetrics.

A good all-round athlete he played both tennis and cricket well and represented the Gentlemen of Ireland. However it was at rugby that he really excelled, playing for Bective Rangers, the Army and the Barbarians.

He was selected to play for Ireland on five occasions between 1913 and 1914. He made his debut against South Africa on 30 November 1912 at Lansdowne Road, Dublin. It didn't go well and they were beaten by thirty-eight points to zero. Not the best of starts to his international career. The following year 1913 he was selected to play in the Five Nations. His first match was against England on 8 February, again at Lansdowne Road. They were to lose again, by four points to fifteen. His next match was against Scotland on 22 February at Inverleith. It was another defeat, this time by twenty-nine points to fourteen. He was selected to play for Ireland in the Five Nations again the following season, 1914. His first match was against England at Twickenham on 14 February, England taking the match by seventeen points to twelve. He made his final first-class appearance against Scotland on 28 February at Lansdowne Road. This time it was a victory by six points to zero, a good end to his international career.

On 15 September 1914, during the First World War, he was commissioned as a lieutenant into the Royal Army Medical Corps, special reserve. He was promoted to captain on 1 April 1915 and saw the war out with that rank, seeing action on the North-West Frontier against the Mohmands and Swatis. He must have enjoyed the life, for on 1 November 1919 he took a regular commission. After the war he remained in India being promoted to major in 1926.

In 1922 he became engaged to Lesley Grogan Anstruther Murray. They married and had one son in 1929.

Between 1930 and 1931 he served in Palestine followed by a year in Malta. In 1938 he was promoted to lieutenant colonel. Between 1938 and 1942 he became the commanding officer of the British Military Hospital in Madras, followed by Wellington, Ranikhet and the prisoner of war camp hospital in India. He died in India on 8 November 1942; the cause of his death is not recorded.

The *Journal of the Royal Army Medical Corps* carried the following obituary to Paddy:

Paddy was one of the real characters of the Corps and the stories of his doings and sayings were many and varied and the recounting of any of them always seemed to draw out the story of a fresh one. Like most Irishmen he was very fond of a horse and did a lot of racing, some of it very successful and most of it amusing, both as an official and an owner in India and Malta. As a rider to hounds he had few superiors, his eye for country, horsemanship and thrust keeping him well to the front. Even in later years, when increasing weight made finding suitable mounts more difficult, he carried on, his beloved Matt sending over suitable animals from Ireland, which Paddy kept at the head of the hunt. At golf he was an amusing companion for anyone who did not take the game too seriously, and at tennis he and his wife were worthy opponents for most people. As a friend Paddy was beyond compare; loyal and affectionate.

He was buried at Delhi War Cemetery, grave reference 6.G.6.

Group Captain Reginald Odbert
Ireland
One test
Royal Air Force
Died 18 July 1943, aged 39
Centre

His life like a fragrant memory, his absence a silent grief

Reginald Vere Massey Odbert (Oddy) was born on 9 February 1904 in Monkstown, Co. Dublin. He was the third son of Herbert Massey Odbert and Annie Emily. He was educated at Blackrock College where he first began to play rugby and Dublin University where he played in their first XV between 1924 and '25. Deciding on a career in the military he took a short service commission in the RAF in June 1907. He played rugby for the RAF and captained the XV in 1928 and 1932.

He made one appearance for Ireland on 29 January 1928 against France at Ravenhill, Belfast. Ireland came out ahead by twelve points to eight. It was to be his only international match.

In 1930-31 he served in Middle East command and between 1934 and 1936 was an experimental pilot in the Armament Testing Squadron. In March 1939, he was appointed to the Directorate of Operational Requirements at the Air Ministry. In June 1936 he was promoted to squadron leader, followed by wing commander in March 1939, and group captain two years later in September 1941.

Odbert died during a gunnery demonstration on Sunday, 18 July 1943, while flying as an observer in Wellington Mk III BK235. The bomber took off from RAF Fulbeck, Lincolnshire, to demonstrate how well gunnery training was going. Several of the inspecting officers who had come to the airfield specially to inspect training flew in the Wellington as observers, including Odbert. The report on the crash was as follows:

> Wellington BK235 was engaged in a corkscrew fighter affiliation exercise on the 18 July 1943 with Martinet HN877 piloted by F/O Jordon. When Jordon was about 200 yards astern of the Wellington he saw the starboard wing of the aircraft break completely off at the outboard of the starboard engine. The Wellington at once went into a dive, and crashed one and half miles south of Appleby, Lincolnshire, killing the six crew members. The crash was timed at 16.25.

Odbert pictured here standing, second from the left in 1928.

The crew was made up of:

Pilot W/O John William Heard RAFVR, aged 21
F/Sgt Daniel Breslin DFM, aged 20
Wing Commander Alister William Stewart Matheson, aged 33
Group Captain Brian Everard Lowe
Squadron Leader Philip Brandon-Trye, aged 24

A brother officer wrote his obituary in *The Times* on 9 August 1943:

In the course of 20 years service in the Royal Air Force men such as Group Captain R. V. M. Odbert acquire many friends. In captaining the rugger team he still further enlarged that circle. All who knew him will agree that 'Oddy' gave his whole life to his profession and closely approached the ideal officer. Those who served with him pay tribute to his honesty of purpose and tenacity: his simplicity of living was exemplary, his only luxury being his generosity to others. These qualities evoked a profound respect both from those who saw eye to eye with him and those who differed in the many difficult problems in which he dealt. After many years of hard work he had his reward. It was clear from talking to his officers and men that during the few months in which he commanded an operational station in Bomber Command they saw in him the man who gave his utmost and who was grateful for the support that inevitably followed. Although he leaves so many friends, there will be many to greet him.

Odbert is commemorated in the Newark-upon-Trent Cemetery, Nottinghamshire, section G, grave 314.

Captain Robert Alexander
Ireland/Great Britain
Fourteen tests
2nd battalion Royal Inniskilling Fusiliers
Died 19 July 1943, aged 32
Flanker

I wished him luck. He paused for a second and whispered to me with a smile,
'It's suicide'

Captain Robert Alexander was born on 24 September 1910 in Belfast. He was educated at the Royal Belfast Academical Institution (RBAI) where he played rugby in the first XV. On leaving the RBAI he went up to Queens University where he was once again in the first XV. He also represented the North of Ireland Football Club (NIFC). Joining the Royal Ulster Constabulary he also played for the Police Union and the Barbarians. He represented the Barbarians on four occasions, twice in 1936 against Newport and Cardiff, and against the same two sides again in 1939.

Alexander represented Ireland and the British Lions on fourteen occasions (eleven times for Ireland and three times for the Lions) between 1936 and 1939. He made his debut for Ireland against England in the Home Nations Championship on 8 February 1936 at Lansdowne Road. It was a great start to his international career as Ireland took the honours by six points to three, Vesey Boyle and Aidan Bailey touching down for Ireland. He appeared next against Scotland at Murrayfield on 22 February. Once again Ireland took the honours by four points to ten, Laurence McMahon and Sam Walker touching down for Ireland and Victor Hewitt dropping a goal. Against Wales on 14 March their run ended when they were beaten by the narrow margin of three points to nil. Wales won the championship with Ireland runners up.

Keeping faith with Alexander he was selected again for the 1937 season. The opening match was against England at Twickenham on 13 February. England edged it by a single point winning the game by nine points to eight. Fred Moran grounded two tries and Aidan Bailey kicked a conversion. Against Scotland on 27 February at Lansdowne Road their luck turned as they defeated Scotland by eleven points to four. It was a memorable game for Alexander as he got the ball across the line and made his first score for his country. Laurence McMahon and Fred Moran scored the other two tries. Aidan Bailey kicked a conversion.

Alexander is seen here, seated on the far right in 1938.

Against Wales on 3 April, at Ravenhill, Ireland came out ahead this time by five points to three, Aidan Bailey grounding a try and Sam Walker kicking the conversion. Once again Ireland were runners up, this time to England.

Alexander was selected for the Home Nations Championship in 1938. The opening match was against England at Lansdowne Road on 12 February. It wasn't a good start as Ireland went down by fourteen points to thirty-six. Aidan Bailey, George Cromey, Maurice Daly and Blair Mayne grounded the tries and Philip Crowe kicked a conversion. It was the same story against Scotland on 26 February at Murrayfield, Scotland winning the game by twenty-three points to fourteen. George Cromey, Fred Moran, George Morgan and David O'Loughlin scored the tries and Sam Walker kicked a conversion. Ireland failed to win a single match during the season and ended up with the wooden spoon with zero points.

Later during the same season (1938) Alexander was selected to go on the British Isles tour of South Africa (the name 'Lions' was not adopted until 1950). The tour party was led by Ireland's Sam Walker and managed by Colonel Hartley and took in 24 matches. Of the 24 games, 19 were against club or invitational teams, three were test matches against South Africans and the other two were outside South Africa against Rhodesia. The British Isles lost two and won one of the test matches, and in other matches lost five and won sixteen. Alexander played in all three matches against South Africa. The first Test was played on 6 August at Ellis Park, Johannesburg. It was a South African victory twenty-six points to twelve. The British managed no tries but Viv Jenkins kicked three penalties and Russell Taylor one. The Second Test was played on 3 September at the Crusaders ground, Port Elizabeth. It was another resounding victory for the South Africans, nineteen points to three. Britain managed to get one try down, scored by Laurie Duff. The final test was played on 10 September at Newlands Stadium, Cape Town. This time it was a different story with Britain taking the match by sixteen points to twenty-one despite being 3-13 down at half time. Alexander was outstanding and scored one of the four tries. Beef Dancer, Laurie Duff and Elfed Jones scored the other three. Harry McKibbin kicked a conversation and a penalty. Charlie Grieve dropped a goal.

Selected to play for Ireland in the 1939 Home Nations Championship, he first took on England at Twickenham on 11 February defeating them zero points to five, John Irwin grounding a try and Harry McKibbin kicking the conversion. His next match was against Scotland at Lansdowne Road. It was another victory this time by twelve points to three. Fred Moran and Desmond Torrens scored a try each, McKibbin kicked a penalty and Mike Sayers managed a goal from a mark (a goal from mark is a former scoring move in rugby. It occurred when a player 'marked' the ball by making a fair catch and shouting 'mark'. From this position the player could not be tackled. The player then had the option of a free kick, which could be taken as a place, drop, or tap kick. The last goal from a mark scored in an international match was by Romania against France in the1971-72 FIRA Nations Cup on 11 December 1971).

Alexander played his final international match on 11 March at Ravenhill, Belfast, against Wales. Alas this result went against them as Ireland lost by zero points to seven. Despite this loss Ireland shared the championship with England and Wales (it was also the last season that France would be excluded following the professionalism arguments in 1931).

During the war Alexander was commissioned into the Royal Inniskilling Fusiliers rising to the rank of captain. He did play one more rugby match, this time captaining an Irish side in a friendly game against the British Army.

Captain Alexander was killed in action near Catania, Sicily on 19 July 1943 while leading his troops in an attack on the Simeto River during the Italian Campaign. A fellow officer David Cole later wrote,

Bob passed me on the way. I wished him luck. He paused for a second and whispered to me with a smile, 'It's suicide', and then went on.

He was right. Alexander together with many of his company were machined-gunned as they attempted to cross the river.

He is buried at the Catania War Cemetery, Sicily, grave reference III.F.1.

Robert Alexander also played one first class cricket match for Ireland against Scotland at Glenpark, Greenock on 18 June 1932. Ireland won by 58 runs (see *The Coming Storm*).

Lieutenant Colonel John Clune
Ireland
Six tests
Royal Army Veterinary Corps
Died 12 September 1942, aged 53
Lock

Died in the infamous Laconia *Incident*

John Joseph Clune was born on 2 April 1890 (some records have it as 21 Jan 1893, in Limerick, but given his age at the time of his death I think the 1890 date is more likely) in Dublin. He was educated at Blackrock College, Dublin, where he first played rugby playing as a hooker/lock and getting into the first XV.

Clune made six appearances for Ireland between 1912 and 1914. He made his debut against South Africa at Lansdowne Road, Dublin, on 30 November 1912. It wasn't a good start as Ireland was trounced 0-38. His next appearance was in the Five Nations against Wales on 13 March 1913 at St Helen's, Swansea. Eight points each at half time, Wales finally edged it in a hard-fought match

Clune can be seen here on the back row, third from the left, as part of the combined Irish and South African teams of 1912.

by sixteen points to thirteen. Joseph Quinn and Albert Stewart got the ball down for Ireland white Richard Lloyd kicked two conversions and a penalty. His next match was against France on 24 March at the Mardyke, Cork. It was a resounding victory for Ireland by twenty-four points to zero. D'Arcy Patterson grounded one try, Joseph Quinn grounded three and William Tyrrell two. Richard Lloyd (captain) kicked three conversions. Despite this victory Ireland finished second from bottom.

Keeping faith with Clune the selectors again decided to play him for the 1914 Five Nations. His first match was against France, played on 1 January 1914 at the Parc des Princes. This time the outcome was much closer but Ireland still managed to take the match by six points to eight despite France being three up at half time. Joseph Quinn and William Tyrrell scored a try each and Richard Lloyd kicked a conversion.

His next match was against England at Twickenham on 14 February. In another hard-fought match England finally took the match by seventeen points to twelve despite Ireland being up by seven points to six at half time. Alexander Foster and Joseph Quinn grounded a try each and Richard Lloyd kicked a conversion and a drop goal.

Clune played his final international match on 14 March 1914 at the Balmoral Showgrounds, Belfast. Wales got the better of the match winning it by three points to eight. Alexander Foster (captain) scored Ireland's only points with a single try.

Attending Dublin University, he trained as a vet, qualifying on 12 December 1917. Clune then took a commission into the Royal Army Veterinary Corps. He was posted to Mesopotamia and served out the war rising to the rank of captain. After the war he served in Kurdistan working at the Veterinary Hospital at Hinaidi, Baghdad and Iraq. He was later posted to India. In 1936 he married Adelaide Kathleen Chichester. Rising to the rank of lieutenant colonel in the Indian Army he served in India during the Second World War.

He was drowned while sailing home on the passenger ship RMS *Laconia* when she was torpedoed off the coast of West Africa on 13 September 1943 taking 1,600 of her passengers down with her. The *Laconia* was carrying 268 British soldiers, 160 Polish soldiers, 80 civilians, and 1,800 Italian prisoners of war. On 12 September 1942 at 8.10 pm, 130 miles north-northeast of Ascension Island, the *Laconia* was hit on the starboard side by a torpedo fired by *U-156*. In the explosion many of the Italian prisoners were killed at once. *Laconia* immediately took a list to starboard and settled heavily by the stern. A second torpedo then hit Number Two hold and Captain Sharp ordered abandon ship. Some of the Italian prisoners then made a rush for the lifeboats. As these were being filled by the women and children (thirty-two of the boats had been destroyed in the explosions) the Polish guards opened fire on them or bayonetted them killing several, but it did restore order. Finally with most of the British and Polish troops away the *Laconia* sank stern first. Only 415 Italians were rescued, out of 1,809 who had been onboard. The other casualties were made up of crew members and Polish and British troops. Alas one of the dead was Lieutenant Colonel John Joseph Clune.

However the plight of the survivors was not yet over and what followed became known as the *Laconia* incident. *U-156* then surfaced and Kapitänleutnant Werner Hartenstein ordered that survivors should be rescued. He also radioed for assistance from other German U-boats in the area. Several arrived, all flying the Red Cross flag to show they were involved in a rescue operation and signalling by radio what they were doing. The following morning an American B-24 spotted them. Hartenstein signalled the aircraft indicating that they were involved in a rescue and asking for assistance. The American pilot radioed the US base in Ascension Island and asked for instructions. The senior American officer there, one Robert C. Richardson III, ordered them to attack the U-boats. The B24 attacked despite the Germans clearly showing Red Cross flags. Despite there being survivors on the decks of the U-boats, they dived to protect themselves and many of their survivors were drowned. After the incident, Admiral Karl Dönitz issued the Laconia Order: henceforth commanders were not to rescue survivors after attacks. About 1,500 people were eventually rescued although some recorders have it as low as 1,083.

Thousands of survivors must have perished thanks to this order. Robert C. Richardson III denied, after the incident, that he was aware that a rescue mission was taking place. However his orders were clearly a war crime under the conventions of war at sea ships. During the time that an enemy submarine is involved in a rescue operation they are no longer lawful objects of attack. The conduct of the aircraft commander appears to be entirely inexcusable, since he must have observed the rescue operation in progress and the Red Cross flags. The fact that the US Army Air Force took no action to investigate this incident, and that no trials took place under the then-effective domestic criminal code, the incident reflects badly on the entire chain of US military command.

Clune is commemorated in the Brookwood Military Cemetery Memorial in Surrey, panel 20, column 2.

His wife Adelaide died on 25 June 1947, aged only 43, at the West Country Hospital, Penzance. She is buried at the Barnoon Cemetery, St Ives.

Major Michael Sayers
Ireland
Ten tests
Royal Artillery
Died 6 December 1943, aged 32
Flanker

Member of the Irish 1935 championship side

Herbert James Michael Sayers was born on 1 May 1911 in Madras, India. He was the son of Sir Frederick Sayers CIE (Companion of the Indian Empire) and of Lady Sayers (née Boyan) of Newtown, Co. Waterford. He was educated at Stonyhurst School where he first played rugby, getting into the first XV. Deciding on a career in the army he went up to Sandhurst. He played for the Army, Lansdowne, Richmond and Surrey. He also represented the Barbarians on four occasions. In 1935 he played against both Cardiff and Newport and in 1942 and 1943 he played against Thorneloe XV.

Sayer is pictured here on the back row, second from the left in 1939.

In great form, he was selected to play for Ireland on ten occasions between 1935 and 1939. He made his debut for Ireland during the 1935 Home National Championships (no longer the Five Nations since France was expelled for professionalism in 1931 – rugby union was amateur at the time) against England at Twickenham on 9 February 1935. In a rather one-sided affair Ireland went down by fourteen points to three, Joseph O'Connor grounding a single try for Ireland. Against Scotland at Lansdowne Road on 23 February it was a different story, with Ireland coming out ahead by twelve points to five despite being down three points to five at half time. Aidan Bailey, Patrick Lawlor, Joseph O'Conor and Ernest Ridgeway all got tries down. Ireland now with their tails up took on Wales at Ravenhill on 9 March, Ireland taking the honours by nine points to three, Jack Doyle getting the only try and Aidan Bailey and Jack Siggins (captain) kicking a penalty each. As a result of their form Ireland won the 1935 championship.

Sayers not surprisingly was selected to play in the Home Championships again in 1936. His first match was against England at Lansdowne Road on 8 February. This time it was Ireland that won the match, by six points to three despite being 3-0 down at half time, Aidan Bailey and Vesey Boyle grounding a try each. Ireland's next match was against Scotland at Murrayfield on 22 February. Once again it was Ireland that played the better rugby and took the match by four points to ten, Laurence McMahon and Sam Walker getting the two tries and Victor Hewitt dropping a goal. In the final match of the season, played against Wales at the National Stadium, Cardiff, on 14 March Wales just pipped them by three points to zero, Viv Jenkins kicking a single penalty to win the game. It was enough to stop them winning the championship for a second year and they were runners up to Wales by just one point.

Sayers missed the 1937 season and only played one match in 1938, against Wales at St Helen's on 12 March. Despite being ahead at half time five points to three, Wales came back at them hard during the second half, taking the match by eleven points to five, Fred Moran grounding a try and Harry McKibbin converting.

The 1939 season saw Sayers playing in all three matches for Ireland. Against England on 11 February at Twickenham, they had a surprise victory by zero points to five, John Irwin grounding a try and Harry McKibbin kicking the conversion. The next match was against Scotland at Lansdowne Road on 25 February. Ireland worked hard and defeated Scotland by twelve points to three, Fred Moran and Desmond Torrens scoring the two tries, Harry McKibbin kicking a penalty and Sayers getting a goal from a mark. They were his first points for Ireland. Sayers' final international came against Wales at Ravenhill on 11 March 1939. Given their form and that the match was being played in Ireland, many saw them as the favourites. However it wasn't to be as Ireland went down by zero points to seven, William Thomas Harcourt Davies scoring both the try and kicking the conversion. Despite this, Ireland still shared the championship with Wales and England.

Sayers was killed in an air accident while a passenger on 6 December 1943. He left a widow, Sheilah Joan, and is buried at Aylesbury Cemetery, Buckinghamshire, section 6, grave 14.

New Zealand

Pilot Officer Donald Cobden
New Zealand
One test
74 Squadron RAF
Died 11 August 1940, aged 26
Wing

One of the few

Donald Cobden was born on 11 August 1914 in Christchurch New Zealand. He was the son of Alfred Palmerston and Mable Elizabeth Cobden of Papanui. He was educated at Christchurch's High School between 1927 and 1931, where he played wing for the first XV. Cobden was tall – 1.83 metres – and powerfully built. He played just twice for Canterbury in 1935 (for a 'B' selection), twice in 1936 and once in 1937. But his size and speed were so impressive he became a contender for the 1937 test series against the touring Springboks. He played in three of the trials and for the South Island before winning All Black selection for the first test against the South Africans.

Cobden pictured in his New Zealand kit in 1937.

The match against the touring Springbok side was, as it turned out, to be his only international match. The match took place on 14 August 1937 at Athletic Park, Wellington. He was one of eight new caps that day and despite the freshness of the team they still came out on top by thirteen points to seven, John Dick grounding a try and David Trevathan kicking two penalties and dropping a goal. Unfortunately Cobden suffered a leg injury due to a bad tackle after twenty-five minutes and was forced to leave the field. His absence meant the All Blacks had to play with fourteen men with wing Ron Ward being moved to Cobden's place. As he was dressed and walking and greeted the team at the end of the game, a national selector said he was outraged and that he should have returned to the field, and proposed to veto his further selection. Alas this proved to be the case, but whether it was because of the selector has never been totally clear.

Cobden is pictured here as part of his squadron, fourth from the left.

In 1937 Cobden left New Zealand and travelled to England, taking a short service commission in the RAF at the end of August 1938. His rugby career in New Zealand had consisted of ten first class matches and one test. For a man of his talents it should have been far more. While Cobden was training as a pilot he found time to play for Catford Bridge, Kent, the RAF and the Barbarians.

After two weeks at Uxbridge he was posted to 5 Flying Training School on 28 January 1939. After training Cobden joined 3 Squadron on 2 September 1939 before moving to 615 Squadron at Croydon on the 8th. On 6 October he was posted to 74 Squadron flying Spitfires at Hornchurch in Essex. The squadron began patrols over France and Belgium on 10 May 1940. On the 24th Cobden shared a Do17, on the 26th he shared a probable Hs126, and on the 27th a probable Do17. Officially the first day of the Battle of Britain, 10 July saw 74 Squadron sent to protect a convoy in the Dover area. In the engagement which followed Cobden got a probable Me109 and damaged a Do17.

On 11 August, 74 took off to patrol convoy 'Booty', twelve miles east of Clacton. In the combat between the Spitfires and forty Me110s, Cobden was last seen attacking a large formation of enemy aircraft. He failed to return from the mission and was posted as missing. Later it was established that he had been shot down and killed on that day, his twenty-sixth birthday.

His body was recovered by the Germans and he is buried in Oostende Communal Cemetery, Belgium, plot 9, row 3, grave 24.

His brother Alf was also killed in action in the Second World War, serving as a gunner with the New Zealand Artillery on 24 October 1942 in North Africa. He also represented Canterbury, between 1933 and '35.

Captain George Fletcher Hart
New Zealand
Eleven tests
20th New Zealand Armoured Corps
Died 3 June 1944, aged 36
Wing

Poetry in motion

George Fletcher Hart was born on 10 February 1909 in Christchurch, New Zealand. He was the son of Leonard Brennan and Emily Hart of Mount Maunganui. He was educated at the Waitaki Boys' High School where he played in the first XV in 1924 and 1925. A fine all-round sportsman, he was also the 1931 New Zealand national 100 yard champion. In 1927 he joined Canterbury and began to play on the wing, where he excelled. He remained with them for eleven seasons and grounded eighty tries during that time, scoring twenty-one tries in a single season. Hart also turned out for Canterbury scoring forty-two tries during his thirty-nine games. He also scored five tries for the South Island.

His speed and talent was not lost on the New Zealand selectors who picked him for the 1930 test against Great Britain (Lions). The match was played on 21 June 1930 at Carisbrook, Dunedin. New Zealand went down by three points to six, with Hart scoring New Zealand's only try and on his debut. One sports commentator said of him after the match:

> He made a fine impression with his change of pace... This deceptive switch remained one of his greatest assets. He would approach a man at full blast, ease off just as his opponent was setting himself for the tackle and then step into top gear again in a swerving burst that was always difficult to counter.

Not surprisingly he was selected for the second test against Great Britain. This time it was a different story. The match was played on 5 July 1930 at Lancaster Park, Christchurch, New Zealand. New Zealand took the match by thirteen points to ten. Hart grounded another try with Don Oliver getting a second and Mark Nicholls kicking two conversions and one goal from the mark. He was selected once again for the third test played at Auckland on 26 July. New Zealand came out on top fifteen points to ten. Although Hart failed to score he played well. Fred Lucas got the ball down once and Hugh McLean twice.

Archie Strang kicked a conversion and Mark Nicholls a drop goal. Hart was played in the forth and final test on 9 August at Athletic Park, Wellington. New Zealand took the match by twenty-two points to eight. Walter Batty and Archie Strang getting one try each while Bert Cooke and Cliff Porter grounded two each. Strang also kicked two conversions.

Despite suffering several injuries, which effected his international career, he remained New Zealand's first choice winger. His next international was played against Australia on 12 September 1931 at Eden, Auckland. Despite being eleven to thirteen at half time, New Zealand fought back to win the match by twenty points to thirteen. Hart managed to get the ball down as did Kelly Ball. Ron Bush kicked a conversion and four penalties.

A caricature of Hart.

Hart had to wait almost three years before being selected again. This time it was during the All Blacks' tour of Australia. The game was played on 11 August 1934 at the Sydney Cricket Ground. Behind at half time six–eleven, New Zealand fought back taking the match by twenty-five points to eleven. Jack Hore, Bubs Knight and Don Max registered a try each with Arthur Collins kicking a conversion.

It was his only international during the 1934 season. He was next selected during New Zealand's tour of Great Britain in 1935. His first match was against Scotland, played on 23 November at Murrayfield, with New Zealand winning eight points to eighteen. Pat Caughey got the ball down three times, while Bill Hadley touched down once. Mike Gilbert kicked three conversions. He next played against Ireland at Lansdowne Road, Dublin, with New Zealand winning once again nine points to seventeen. Hart managed to ground one try, as well as Brushy Mitchell and Charlie Oliver. Mike Gilbert kicked one conversion and two penalties. On 21 December he ran out against Wales at the National Stadium, Wales. In a close-run match Wales managed to overcome the mighty New Zealand by thirteen points to twelve. Kelly Ball scored two tries, while Mike Gilbert kicked a conversion and a drop goal.

In 1936 Hart was selected to play against the visiting Australians. Hart's first match was played on 5 September 1936 at Athletic Park, Wellington, with New Zealand winning by eleven points to six. Hart managed a try as did Bill Hadley and Jim Watt; Bunk Pollock kicked a conversion. Hart made his final international appearance on 12 September against Australia at Carisbrook, Dunedin. It was a good end to an outstanding career, New Zealand taking the match by thirty-eight points to thirteen. Hart grounded two tries as did Brushy Mitchell, Jack Rankin and Tori Reid. Jim Watt got a further try. Bunk Pollock kicked four conversions and one penalty. In total Hart played for the All Blacks thirty-five times, including eleven internationals and scoring a total of twenty-eight tries. Hart retired from international and provincial rugby in 1936 and moved to Tauranga.

Former All Black player and coach Jim Burrows later said of Hart in his autobiography, *Pathway Among Men*,

> He could ignite a crowd running down the side-line like a wild deer. The crowd knowing exactly what was going to happen would wait for him to veer infield, then watch the opposing fullback check his pace and would roar with delight as George would veer out again and race around to score.

Hart married Maisie Chambers Hart of Mission Bay Auckland.

Hart served with the 2nd New Zealand Expeditionary Force during the Second World War, becoming a captain with the 20th Armoured Corps. During this time he continued to play rugby for the New Zealand Army including the match against the South African Springboks team while posted in Egypt. He died of wounds on 3 June 1944 after being hit by a shell on the advance to Rome after the battle at Monte Cassino. He actually died in a Catholic seminary in Soro, north of Monte Cassino, which had previously been used as a German hospital. His surgeon was Captain Walter Irving Cawkwell. He is buried in the Cassino War Cemetery, grave reference X.H.12.

Scotland

Pilot Officer Donald Mackenzie
Scotland
Two tests
603 Squadron RAF
Died 12 June 1940, aged 23
Number 8

First rugby international killed during the Second World War

Donald Kenneth Andrew Mackenzie was born on 30 November 1916 in China. He was the son of John, a customs officer in Shanghai, and Bertha. The family later returned to Edinburgh. Mackenzie was educated at the Inverness Academy where he trained to be an accountant. Mackenzie's club side was Edinburgh Wanderers, where he developed quickly and came to the notice of the Scottish selectors. He was picked to play for Scotland twice, both caps coming during Scotland's disastrous 1939 season. Scotland entered the season as Triple Crown champions, having beaten all three of their opponents in the 1938 Home

SCOTLAND 1939
Scotland 3 - Ireland 12 - Dublin - 25th February 1939

J R S Innes   R B Bruce Lockhart   I N Graham   D K A Mackenzie   I C Henderson   W Purdie   C H Gadney (Referee)
A Roy   D J Macrae   K C Fyfe   R W Shaw (Captain)   G B Horsburgh   W B Young   G D Shaw
T F Dorward   W M Penman

Scotland

Nations championship. The Grand Slam was not available as France had been banned from competing over allegations of professionalism. Scotland would lose all three of their 1939 games, ending bottom of the table as England, Wales and Ireland finished joint top with two victories each.

Mackenzie was brought in at No. 8 for the second match of the season, against Ireland, replacing the redoubtable Laurie Duff who had recently played two tests for the British Lions in South Africa. Scotland had lost the opener in Wales and were away again, finding themselves playing on a filthy day in Dublin. They had hoped to capitalise on their mesmeric backline, which had wreaked so much havoc in the Triple Crown season. They had put twenty-three points past Ireland that year, but the weather and a brilliant display from the Irish pack put pay to any hopes of a repeat. The Scots tried hard, having been accused of capitulating in the Welsh game, but simply could not compete with the 'lusty forward rushes' which typified the Irish play.

In its match report, *The Scotsman* was generous to Mackenzie, stating, 'The new cap DKA Mackenzie also did well and was particularly prominent in the opening stages' before adding the slightly cryptic note that 'his fine height was not only useful but necessary.'

Mackenzie kept his place for the season's final match, against England at Murrayfield. The match was another disappointment. A record crowd arrived at Murrayfield hoping for a repeat of the previous season's victory at Twickenham where Wilson Shaw had inspired his team to a famous victory with two scintillating tries. The Scottish captain responded with his best performance of a mediocre season, crossing for one of his team's two scores. However, whereas in 1938 the Scottish backs had been good enough to compensate for a badly beaten pack, there would be no such escape on this occasion. The Scottish forwards lost 48 scrums and 21 line outs, winning only 12 and 8 respectively, with *The Scotsman* opining that 'seldom has an international pack been so outplayed.' The English forwards were hardly stretched, dominating play even more comprehensively than the statistics suggest. The back row were singled out for special criticism, with *The Scotsman* writing 'DKA Mackenzie was amongst the men who was hardly seen.' The newspaper also reported how his back row colleague W.H. Crawford 'suffered the unusual distinction of being told from the embankments what he ought to do.'

Given the inadequacy of both his individual performance and that of the team, Mackenzie may well not have played for Scotland again. The outbreak of war was to make that an academic question. Mackenzie was a member of the Auxiliary Air Force, a reserve of civilian pilots trained and ready to serve the country in time of conflict. In 1939 Pilot Officer Mackenzie and his squadron, 603 (City of Edinburgh) were transferred to the full-time RAF.

The squadron was strategically placed to defend Scotland's industrial heartlands and the approaches to the great naval base at Scapa Flow. On 16 October 1939 the unit claimed the war's first German victim over British soil, a Junkers 88 bomber.

603 Squadron was equipped with Spitfires, having been recently upgraded from Gloster Gladiator biplanes. Mackenzie was piloting Spitfire L1050 on a training flight on 12 June 1940 when it crashed during a night exercise near Balerno, eight miles south-west of Edinburgh. He was killed outright.

Mackenzie's squadron flew south two months after his death to take part in the Battle of Britain. Helped by pilots such as 'ace' Brian Carvery and Richard Hillary, author of *The Last Enemy*, 603 would claim more German aircraft than any other squadron in the battle.

Mackenzie is commemorated in the Colinton Parish Churchyard, southern extension, section N, grave 14.

Pilot Officer Thomas Dorward
Scotland
Five tests
25 Squadron Royal Air Force Volunteer Reserve
Died 5 March 1941, aged 24
Scrum half

'A really good scrum half'

Tom or 'Tommy' Dorward was born on 27 March 1916 in Galashiels, Scotland. He was the second son of the Galashiels textile manufacturer Adam Paterson and Isabella Fairgrieve Dorward of Galashiels. Along with his brothers Pat and Arthur, he attended Sedbergh School. Sedbergh sits in the sort of dramatic Cumbrian scenery to be expected of the school attended by William Wordsworth's son. It has an educational approach which matches the rugged scenery and is epitomised in the school motto: *A Stern Nurse of Men*.

The school's ethos clearly suited the Dorward brothers, with all three performing well academically and on the playing fields. Despite the often inclement weather – the school's meteorological society doggedly recorded 80 inches of rain in 1928, with up to 3.5 inches falling in one day – cricket was a priority in the summer. Tom was described as being cheerful in fielding practice and, overall, 'a very fair player, with a weakness for playing straight bowling to square leg'.

The major sport was, of course, rugby. The Dorward boys all played to a high level, with Arthur later joining Tom on the school's impressive list of international players. Names such as John Spencer, Will Carling, Will Greenwood and James Simpson-Daniel will resonate with modern readers. At the time of Tom's attendance, however, the name of William Wavell Wakefield stood head and shoulders above the others on the list.

Wakefield was a true polymath. His rugby career saw him win thirty-one caps and inspire England to back-to-back grand slams in 1923 and '24. He is credited as being one of the game's finest thinkers and strategists, and went on to become president of the RFU. Outside rugby he served with distinction in both the First and Second World Wars, was a long-standing Conservative politician, and found time to be influential in the development of both scuba diving and ski jumping.

Wakefield remained closely connected with the affairs of the school, regularly playing in Old Boys' matches during Tom's time. In a match just before Christmas 1933 Tom was playing for the school against the legendary flanker, the school journal gleefully recording the moment: 'WW Wakefield successfully dummied half the side'.

Tom was quickly established as the scrum half for the first XV, and benefitted from the high standard of rugby played there. In 1933 he played in the annual fixture against Loretto School where he was in opposition to the winger W.N. Renwick. Renwick would go on to play alongside Dorward for Scotland in 1938 and was also destined to die in the war.

The Sedberghian praised Tom as a 'really good scrum half' and in 1935 wrote, 'Dorward was outstanding, being very quick off the mark and armed with the most convincing dummy' – it appears he was paying attention when playing against the great man!

Dorward's partner at fly half was Rab Bruce Lockhart, a pairing that was to be recreated at national level in 1939. Bruce Lockhart was a scion of the Scottish sporting, teaching and spying family. Rab's father, John, was Sedbergh's headmaster and himself a dual cricket-rugby international. Rab's brother Logie also played rugby for Scotland. John's brother, Robert, was a noted footballer and worked for the British secret service while serving as unofficial ambassador to the Bolsheviks in 1917!

Tom left Sedbergh in 1935 and returned to the Borders where he became a fixture in the Gala side. He rapidly attracted the attention of the regional selectors and October of that year saw him facing the All Blacks in their tour match against the South of Scotland. The 1935 team was not quite the match of New Zealand's two previous touring parties (the 1905 *Originals* and the 1924 *Invincibles* who between them had one – disputed – loss in seventy-two matches), but to the Borders public the All Blacks were still the All Blacks. 11,000 were at Hawick's ground to see the game.

The match was very nearly a historic victory for the Scottish side. The occasion was noted for the 'robust' competition between the forwards and Tom will have had a good view of the shenanigans from his vantage point at scrum half. The Borderers refused to be intimidated, and indeed took the game to the All Blacks – bewildering the Kiwis with a fine dribbling display. The south were in the lead with ten minutes to go, but conceded late points and then missed a final penalty which would have given them a draw.

Clearly Tom could hold his own against the strongest competition. By 1937 he was in contention for the Scottish team. He was invited to play for F.J.C. Moffat's invitation team in a specially arranged match against Watsonians, apparently to see how he fared against the home side's equally promising scrum half. In the end neither player was able to oust the Scottish captain

Ross Logan from his position in the side. Tom had to wait until 1938 for his debut.

The 1938 season was a famous one for Scotland. The Triple Crown was won for the eighth time in the nation's history, a feat that would not be repeated for forty-six years. The achievement was no less sweet for being in some ways a notional one. In keeping with the strict amateur ethos of the time, the Home Nations championship was, officially, merely a series of friendly matches. A trophy for what had become the Six Nations championship did not arrive until 1993, and the Triple Crown had to wait until 2006. Scotland have yet (2017) to be awarded the physical trophy.

Dorward made his international debut against Wales at Murrayfield on 5 February 1938. Despite being 0-6 down at half time Scotland fought back hard, to finally take the game by the narrow margin of eight points to six, Wilf Crawford scoring all the points with a try, a conversion and a penalty. His next match was against Ireland, again at Murrayfield, on 26 February. Once again Scotland took the honours by twenty-three points to fourteen. Archibald Drummond scored one try and kicked a penalty, John Forrest got the ball down twice and Duncan Macrae managed a fourth try. Wilf Crawford kicked two conversions and Dorward got off his international mark by dropping a goal. Scotland's final match of the season was against the old enemy England at Twickenham. The match was played on 19 March. Scotland played a brilliant game beating England by sixteen points to twenty-one. Charles Dick scored Scotland's opening try, William Renwick grounded two further tries and Wilson Shaw two more. Wilf Crawford kicked two penalties. Scotland would only defeat England at Twickenham on four occasions during the entire twentieth century. The game is known as Wilson Shaw's Match in honour of Scotland's mercurial captain.

Dorward was selected to play for Scotland again during the 1939 season. His first match was against Ireland at Lansdowne Road on 25 February. This time Ireland beat Scotland by twelve points to three, Donny Innes getting Scotland's only points with a try.

Dorward's final international match was played against England at Murrayfield on 18 March. In a close game England finally emerged as winners by six points to nine, William Murdoch and Wilson Shaw grounding a try each. On both occasions he was partnered by his old Sedbergh team mate Bruce Lockhart. This may have provided some personal satisfaction but the

SCOTLAND 1939

Scotland 3 - Ireland 12 - Dublin - 25th February 1939

J R S Innes   R B Bruce Lockhart   I N Graham   D K A Mackenzie   I C Henderson   W Purdie   C H Gadney (Refe
A Roy   D J Macrae   K C Fyfe   R W Shaw (Captain)   G B Horsburgh   W B Young   G D Shaw
T F Dorward   W M Penman

national side endured a miserable season, the Triple Crown champions being whitewashed in the last championship before the war, as well as losing 11-3 to Wales.

Perhaps again inspired by Wavell Wakefield, Tom signed up for the RAF. While in the service he continued to find time for rugby, as when playing alongside fourteen other internationals for Bob Oakes' Traditional XV against West Hartlepool in April 1940.

In 1941 he was engaged to be married. On 5 March of that year he was piloting L6602 – a Mark 1F Bristol Blenheim – between RAF Wittering and RAF Digby. It crashed, killing him and his signals officer John Austin Strong. The accident report is poignant in its brevity:

Collided with tree during low level daylight flight in intermittent fog conditions and crashed into the ground near Cottesmore, Rutland.

Thomas Dorward is commemorated in the Galashiels (Eastland) Cemetery, grave reference, section B.5, Grave 2.

Sergeant (Pilot) William Alexander Ross
Scotland
Two tests
55 Squadron RAFVR
Died 28 September 1941, aged 28
Fly half

Ross's bravery was admired by Rommel himself

William Alexander Ross was born on 15 November 1913 in Glasgow. He was the son of Jean Lang Ross of Hillhead, Glasgow. Ross attended Glasgow Hillhead School and later played for the school's former pupils side. He gained his caps for Scotland in the 1937 season. Surprisingly, he was the only player from that season to be amongst the fourteen Scottish internationals to die in the Second World War.

Ross was one of seven debutants who started the first match against Wales in Cardiff. The previous international season had been something of a disaster for Scotland, who finished bottom of the table without winning a single game. 1937 at least got off to a better start, with the team winning 13-6. Ross played as fly half, partnered by Ross Logan at scrum half. The Scottish backs on that day included Charles Dick and the great Wilson Shaw.

Dick was a fine rugby player and a distinguished physician. Born in Sevenoaks of Scottish parents he was eligible to play for both Scotland and England. Scotland were quick to offer him a trial and thereafter a place in the team. He would go on to win fourteen caps, with notable achievements including a try against the All Blacks and membership of the scintillating back line which won the 1938 Triple Crown. Having emigrated to New Zealand he was appointed the Queen's honorary physician in 1958.

SCOTLAND 1937

Scotland 13 - Wales 6 - Swansea - 6th February 1937

M M Henderson   D J Macrae   G B Horsburgh   C L Melville   W M Inglis   G L Gray
W G S Johnston   R W Shaw   R C S Dick   W R Logan   J A Waters   W B Young   G D Shaw
J M Kerr   W A Ross

Ross missed the second match of the season, a defeat by Ireland, but was back in the side for the final match, against England. Once again Scotland were beaten, with Sever and Unwin scoring a try each for England, answered only by a penalty from G.D. Shaw. England thus won their eleventh Triple Crown and thirteenth title. Scotland at least had the consolation of avoiding the wooden spoon, which was awarded to Wales who had lost all of their matches.

The selectors again rang the changes for the next season, with the first match in 1938 seeing no less than eight new caps. Ross would not play for his country again. An accountant by profession, he was also a member of the Royal Air Force Volunteer Reserve – joining up full-time at the outbreak of war.

By 1941 Ross was stationed at Fuka aerodrome in northern Egypt. Possession of the airfield alternated between the Allied and Axis forces throughout the North African conflict. At this point in the campaign the Allies were trying to stop the advance of Rommel's Africa Korps, who had themselves reversed earlier Italian losses. In November 1942 the Allies would finally settle the matter with victory at El Alamein.

On the morning of 28 September 1941 Ross was detailed to attack a German fuel ship. His Bristol Blenheim V5560 took off at 0407 for the low-level attack on a 2,000-ton German ship in Bardia Harbour. The attack was made at sea level and as the aircraft turned away after dropping its bombs it was hit by flak and crashed into a small house, killing the three crew members, William Ross, Sergeant Charles Ian Johnson (RNZAF), Ernest James Sprange (RAFVR) and several German soldiers.

The attack was witnessed by Gernot Knop, an engineer in the Afrika Korps. In 2010 the *Daily Mail* revealed how Knop gathered together the Scot's possessions and, after the war, sent them to his fiancée Dorothy Bird, using an address found amongst the possessions. Knop described how Ross's plane had passed no more than ten metres above them, with Ross directing his gunner's fire until the very end. Ross's bravery was apparently admired by Rommel himself and he was buried with military honours.

Among Ross's few possessions recovered from the crash site was a copy of the team photograph from the March 1937 match against England.

He is commemorated in the Halfaya Sollum War Cemetery, grave 4.D.9-10.

Private Patrick Munro MP
Scotland
Thirteen tests
1st County of London Battalion, Home Guard
Died 3 May 1942, aged 58
Half back

Killed in training accident with the Home Guard

Patrick Munro was born on 9 October 1883 in Knaresborough. He was the eighth child and fifth son of Patrick Munro, secretary of a life assurance company, and his wife, Mary Helen Catherine Dormond. Patrick was educated at Leeds Grammar School before going up to Christ Church College, Oxford. It was his athletic ability that made him exceptional. The Varsity match may then have functioned as an unofficial international trial, but it was still unusual for an undergraduate to amass, as Munro did, ten caps. He was also awarded a half-blue for his prowess as a long jumper.

Leadership obviously came naturally to the young Munro, as he was captain for the last of his three rugby blues and held the prestigious position of Vincent's Club President in 1907. The club was formed by W.B. Woodgate in 1863 with the intention of identifying an elite among the university's undergraduates, who were 'selected for all-round qualities: social, physical and intellectual qualities being duly considered'. Most members were blues.

By the time he attained the Vincent's presidency Munro was already a Calcutta Cup winner, had faced the mighty All Blacks and defeated the Springboks. During his tenure he would be made captain of his country, defeat Ireland and once again capture the Calcutta Cup. Even in this elite amongst the elite, Munro's precocious sporting talent stood out. He was a natural choice for president.

His first season as an international, 1904/05, had been an indifferent one for the Scots, an 8-0 victory over England at Richmond being the only success. Scotland were beaten 12-7 by the All Blacks and, like the other home nations, were shocked by the quality of play displayed by the first New Zealand team to tour Britain. Cosy notions of domestic superiority over the 'dominions' were shattered by Dave Gallaher and his men. Only Wales managed to beat the *Originals* in a tour of thirty-five matches – and that result is hotly disputed in New Zealand to this day.

Scotland

W L Russell	T Sloan	L M Macleod	K G Macleod	L L Greig	J C MacCallum	J G Scoular
J M Mackenzie	J T Simson	W P Scott	D R B Sivright	L West	W E Kyle	E D Simson
					P Munro	

The 1905/06 season was another mixed bag for Scotland, with losses to Wales and England bracketing a win over Ireland. Munro at least had the compensation of scoring his first points for his country – a try in the Irish match.

The 1906/07 season was anything but mediocre, and indeed was viewed by some contemporaries as 'the most successful season in Scotland's thirty-six-year rugby history'. The outstanding result was a 6-0 defeat of South Africa in front of 32,000 spectators at Hampden Park in November. The Springboks may not have been quite as good as the All Blacks, but they only lost twice in twenty-nine games and Scotland were the only national team to beat them on the tour.

Munro did not play in the next match, a victory against Wales, but he was installed as captain for the visit of Ireland on 23 February. The Irish were defeated, as were the English, in a game played at Blackheath, leaving Munro captain of a Triple Crown winning side and celebrating Scotland's eighth outright title.

Munro was posted to Sudan in the first stage of a distinguished diplomatic career, centred in East Africa. He progressed through the ranks and would eventually serve as governor of both Darfur (1923-4) and Khartoum (1925-9). As a colonial administrator, Munro had wide-ranging powers of administration and justice. He was responsible for great ranges of inhospitable territory, which usually had to be crossed on horseback. He seems to have met these challenges with a mixture of humour and physical endurance, endearing him to those he governed. He reputedly gave his international cap to a tribal chief, who wore it instead of his fez on state occasions.

By 1911 Munro had temporarily returned to London, where he played for London Scottish. One match took the side to the newly-opened Twickenham stadium to play Harlequins. Despite being based only a few miles away in Richmond the Anglo-Scots got thoroughly lost trying to gain access to the new-fangled stadium. Both Munro and George (later Sir George) Cunningham – a fellow international and diplomat – had to make an undignified entrance through the surrounding allotments and over the fence.

In 1910 the Five Nations championship had been born, with France joining England, Ireland, Scotland and Wales. The home nations had, somewhat reluctantly, overcome their doubts as to the amateur status of the French game.

Munro was selected as captain for the first match of the 1911 international season, picking up where he had left off four years before. The man he replaced as both captain and fly half (or half back, the terminology was still fluid) was none other than his friend George Cunningham. The match was against France at Stade Colombes. Munro scored a try, but *Les Bleus* secured a win by 16-15, their first ever win in the championship.

There was a horrified reaction to the result in Scotland, with the result widely taken as a misprint. The following two matches were home contests against Wales and Ireland. Munro contributed a drop goal in each game, but could not prevent two more losses. His international career thus came to an undistinguished end, and he was not selected for the final match – against England at Twickenham.

Munro returned to Africa to continue his diplomatic service, having married Jessie Margaret Martin in October 1911.

He served in the First World War, where he was mentioned in dispatches.

By 1931 he had returned to Britain, and was elected MP for Llandaff and Barry, holding the seat until his death.

Munro was 55 at the outbreak of war and volunteered for service as a private in the Home Guard. In May 1942 he was taking part in an exercise when a bomb exploded and he was killed.

He is commemorated in Cathedine (St Michael) Churchyard, where he had a home.

Second Lieutenant James Ritchie
Scotland
Six tests
14th Battalion, 1st Punjab Regiment
Died 6 July 1942, aged 34
Hooker

He excelled at everything

James McPhail Ritchie was born on 10 July 1907 in Edinburgh. He was the son of the late Mr John S. Ritchie of Bruntsfield Place and Mrs Ritchie of 12 Bruntsfield Gardens, Edinburgh. Bruntsfield Place is only a short walk from the original site of George Watson's College, the famous sporting school which Ritchie attended between 1912 and 1923. The Archibald Road site was in the city centre and pupils had to travel several miles to the school's Myreside sports ground.

Fortunately Edinburgh at that time was free from traffic congestion and benefitted from an extensive and cheap tram service. Ritchie, awarded his school colours for both cricket and rugby, must have been a frequent traveller on the Nos 9 and 10 trams which linked the two sites.

As well as rugby and cricket Ritchie excelled at water polo, at which he also represented his country. To follow this activity the energetic young Ritchie would have been required to take a number 6 or 18 tram to the beautiful Warrender Baths. This famous Victorian building is still (2017) open to all and is now best known for having produced David Wilkie, breast stroke gold medallist at the 1976 Olympics. At the time it was home to the all-conquering Warrender Wanderers water-polo team. Ritchie was the team's captain.

It may be fair to surmise that the young Ritchie excelled more on the sports field than in the classroom. Instead of continuing his studies at university, as might have been expected for a gifted athlete at such a school, he left education at 16 and joined the city's Century Insurance Company. Located in Charlotte Square (in the heart of Edinburgh's financial district and well served by numerous trams) the company was in the midst of a period of expansion, having been bought by Friends Provident. Century was experimenting in the new sphere of motor insurance as well as branching out overseas.

Ritchie continued to play rugby for Watsonians while working for Century, being elected captain of the club in 1934. He had to wait for ten years after leaving school, however, to gain his first international rugby cap – a long wait in an era when international careers begun early. Perhaps Ritchie was paying the price for not having attended university, Varsity teams providing a conventional route to the national side.

At this time Scotland's only internationals were in the Home Nations Championship. After a brief period as the Four Nations the competition had reverted to its original membership with the expulsion of France over suspected professionalism, France would not be readmitted until after the Second World War. Following England's 'Golden Era' in the period before and after the Great War, the championship was undergoing an indeterminate period with no country dominating and the title often being shared.

Ritchie made his debut against Wales on 4 February 1933. Scotland won the game, and would go on to secure the championship and Triple Crown with victories over England and Ireland. This was Scotland's first clean sweep since Phil Macpherson's men had won the country's first ever Grand Slam in 1925, securing the triumph with a victory over England in the match which marked the opening of Murrayfield Stadium.

Since the debut match Murrayfield had become something of a stronghold for the Scots, who won their first seven games against England at the stadium.

SCOTLAND 1933

Scotland 3 - England 0 - Edinburgh - 18th March 1933

Dr J R Wheeler	K L T Jackson	J R Thom	J M Ritchie	J M Henderson	H B D Lorraine	D I Brown
W R Logan	R Rowand	W B Welsh	I S Smith , Captain	J Beattie	M S Stewart	J A Waters
		H Lind		K C Fyfe		

Scotland

The 1933 game was won by the narrowest possible margin, 3-0, the points being secured by Ken Fyfe's try. The scoring rules at the time meant that England could have rescued a victory at any time with a drop goal, which was then worth four points and the most valuable score in the game.

The next season, 1934, was less successful for Scotland. Playing at prop, although he is recorded elsewhere as a hooker – player specialisation was less rigid in those days – Ritchie was once again an ever-present. The first match was lost at home to Wales, by six points to thirteen. The match saw Ritchie score his only international points, a penalty which was added to a try by the scrum half Logan.

The Welsh result was a serious disappointment after the successes of the previous season, but was perhaps unsurprising given that the selectors chose eight debutants in the side. Selectorial whim and 'Buggins' turn' were a frustrating reality for players of this era, but this was excessive by any standards. A mere four debuts were announced for the subsequent Irish game, and the selectors were rewarded for their comparative restraint. A fine 16-9 victory featured one try by John Crawford (on debut) and a brace from Dick.

Ritchie's final match was against England at Twickenham. The selectors made only one change, bringing Ken Fyfe back in place of the unlucky Crawford – who had played his one and only international game. Perhaps stunned by this display of consistency the Scots were beaten in another low-scoring game. Two tries by Booth and Meikle gave England six points to the three gained by Wilson Shaw's score for Scotland. It was to be the first of five tries Wilson Shaw scored against England, including two in the famous Triple Crown winning match of 1938.

During this time he met and married Evelyn Ritchie of West Newport Fife. They had one son Gordon.

The end to Ritchie's international career was caused by his joining the Calcutta manufacturing company Bird & Co. He remained in India until the outbreak of the war, serving as a captain in the 14th Battalion, 1st Punjabi Regiment.

By July 1942 the situation in India was critical, with the Japanese army approaching through Burma. Ritchie was in Rawalpindi (now in Pakistan), one of almost a million troops preparing to defend the Raj. It was monsoon season, which stopped the Japanese advance but also brought devastating health problems for the tightly-packed troops. It was to the water-borne typhoid fever that Ritchie succumbed, dying on the 16th of that month.

The Glasgow Herald carried the following obituary on 16 July 1942:

Final Scrum

The death has occurred at Rawalpindi, India, of Captain J.M. Ritchie, Indian Army, who played in the Scottish International rugby team as a forward throughout the 1933 and 1934 series of games. Captain Ritchie, who was educated at Watson's College, was also a water polo internationalist, while as a cricketer he had considerable gifts as a fast bowler for the Watsonians.

Ritchie is commemorated in the Rawalpindi War Cemetery, grave reference 2.A.4.

Scotland

Lieutenant John Forrest
Scotland
Three tests
Royal Naval Volunteer Reserve
Died 14 September 1942, aged 25
Wing

Strathallan School
Archive.

Killed in Spitfire training flight

John Gordon Scott Forrest was born on 28 April 1917 in Rhodesia and educated at Strathallan School in Perthshire between 1931 and 1936. It cannot have been easy for other sporting boys at the school, as Forrest carried all before him. As might be expected of a future international, he was captain of the rugby side for two years. The summers saw him given the same honour in the cricket team, with 1936 seeing him average 96.1 with the bat and take 29 wickets at 8.6 runs each. He was tennis champion, captain of the swimming team and more than useful at water polo and fives.

Forrest's most remarkable achievement however came on the athletics field. He swept the board in both of his final years at the school, winning the 110 yards, the 220, the quarter mile, the 880, the 120 yard hurdles, the high jump and throwing the cricket ball on the same afternoon, and setting four school records.

Forrest was given the nickname 'Springy', presumably in tribute to his athletic abilities. He also gained the reputation for modesty and decency that was to follow him throughout his life. As he left to study medicine, the school magazine said of him, 'the prowess of JGS Forrest on the playing field dwarfs everything in school history.'

Cambridge was to provide Forrest's next sporting challenge. At the time, university rugby was genuinely high class, and a recognised route to the national sides. Forrest's pedigree was quickly identified, and he was given the rare honour of gaining his blue during his freshman year. By December 1938 he was an established international player and captain of the Cambridge side, taking a team containing seven other Scots to Twickenham for the Varsity match.

Befitting its status, the match against Oxford was given widespread media coverage. *The Dundee Courier* headlined its report 'Twickenham Hero was JGS

141

Forrest is pictured in these two photographs centrally in the middle row. *Strathallan School Archive.*

Forrest' and talked of his 'genius' before detailing how his thrilling run had set up fellow international Bruce Lockhart for the winning try.

The match was also notable for a thundering tackle between Forrest and his opposing captain. H.D. Freakes, the Oxford skipper, had been born in South Africa but had already played for England. Given Forrest's Rhodesian background there was perhaps an element of southern hemisphere competition between the two internationals. Whatever the reason, the tackle lived long in the memory of those who witnessed it.

By the time of this, his last, Varsity appearance Forrest's international career had already finished.

All three of his caps came during Scotland's triumphant Triple Crown season of 1938. His debut came against Wales and he seemed to get off to an indifferent start (the players were distracted by a dog who wouldn't leave the pitch), before finding his form in the second half and running 'splendidly' to set up Crawford for the decisive try. He scored two tries in the comprehensive victory over Ireland which followed the Welsh match, before moving on to the decisive encounter at Twickenham on 19 March.

This match saw Scotland secure a glorious victory on a sunny afternoon in front of the king and queen. George VI may not have been as much of a rugby man as his father, George V, but he cannot have failed to enjoy the spectacle provided by Forrest and his fellow Scottish backs. Inspired by their captain Wilson Shaw, but playing behind a defeated pack, the Scots scored five tries and won the game by twenty-one points to sixteen. George's queen, known to future generations as 'The Queen Mother', showed her heritage with enthusiastic backing for the Scots.

The Scotsman reported how 'Forrest really played a great game, tackling strongly, running well and being ever ready to back up Shaw's excursions into the enemy territory... I think Forrest will become one of our great players.'

Events were to deny Forrest the opportunity to fulfil this potential. He was injured or unavailable for selection during Scotland's disappointing 1939 season. By this time he appears to have already been serving as a fighter pilot in the RNVR. He is recorded as having played for Portsmouth as early as 1937 (while still at university) and in March 1939 was playing for the United Services team.

In 1941 Forrest was serving with 880 Naval Squadron, successively based on the carriers *Furious*, *Indomitable* and *Eagle*. Known to his shipmates as 'Johnnie' he saw service as far north as the Arctic and as far south as Madagascar. The unit also travelled to the United States and fought alongside three other carriers during Operation Pedestal, the vital August 1942 convoy to resupply Malta.

After the trauma of Pedestal, Forrest and his fellow pilots returned to Liverpool aboard HMS *Indomitable*. They had a short period of leave and were then re-equipped, with Seafires (the marine equivalent of Spitfires) replacing their Sea Hurricanes. During formation practice on 14 September 1942, while flying Spitfire VB (AB873) based at HMS Blackcap, Forrest collided with another Spitfire (BL 487) piloted by Sub-Lieutenant Popham near Altrincham. The collision took place at 7,000 feet and Popham managed to bail out and survive, but the gallant Forrest crashed at Pownall Green Farm and was killed.

Dai Gent (Gloucester and England) wrote in *The Sunday Times*:

Rugby men everywhere will have read with deep regret of the death in action of that grand Scots international three-quarter J.G.S. Forrest, R.N. Air Arm. No matter whether he was in the centre or on the wing, every time he pulled more than his weight. I saw his Freshman's match at Cambridge. He was not in either team as they lined out but, upon a centre having to go off crocked, Forrest came on to take his place. It was seen in the twinkling of an eye that Cambridge had here a 'find'. He never looked back, got his blue as a Fresher, and from that, my first view of him to my last when I saw him get a try 'in a hundred' last year at Taunton he never gave a bad or a poor game in my seeing. He and H.D. Freakes, the two mighty opposites in a well-remembered tackle in a Varsity match, when both were in the centre, have now made the great sacrifice, lamented by all who ever knew them or only saw them play.

The Scotsman wrote on Tuesday, 29 September:

Forrest was a magnificent player, whether on the wing or in the centre. I preferred him in the centre, where his running and serving and side-stepping and kicking and passing gave me no end of pleasure; and I am sure that in this modest and charming young Scotsman we have lost a great rugby footballer in the making.

Forrest is commemorated in Paisley (Woodside) Crematorium Cemetery memorial, on panel 2.

969712 Flight Sergeant Roy Kinnear
Scotland & British Lions
Seven tests
RAFVR (Flight Engineer)
Died 22 September 1942, aged 38
Centre

Father of the British character actor Roy Kinnear
Died playing rugby

Roy Muir Kinnear was born on 3 February 1904 in Edinburgh, the son of Robert Mitchell and Agnes Kinnear. Kinnear attended George Heriot's School in Edinburgh between 1916 and 1922. He excelled on the rugby pitch from an early age, being described in the school journal as 'the star performer of the team… his high step and determined running make him difficult to tackle. Adept at evading a speedier pursuer. He has no equal as a centre at any Scottish School.'

Heriot's first XV played nineteen matches in Roy's final season at the school, winning seventeen with only a single loss and one draw. There was then nothing as vulgar as a league for rugby matches between Scottish public schools, but this was a successful season by anybody's standards. *The Herioter* school magazine summed them up as 'a great side', and was particularly impressed by the team's 'assiduous practice and fine team spirit'.

On leaving Heriot's Roy began to play for the school's former pupils' side, which at the time regularly turned out six teams. The rugby played was of a high quality. That season the great Heriot's fullback Dan Drysdale would win the first of his twenty-six Scottish caps, and would later become the first pupil from the school to captain his country. Drysdale was one of the driving forces behind a successful period for Scotland, winning eighteen out of his twenty-six games across six years. Lining up alongside Drysdale and Kinnear for Heriot's was K.G.P. Hendrie – another future international.

Kinnear was clearly not overawed to be playing in such company. In his first season his scores included tries against Royal High Schools FP, Glasgow Academicals, Glasgow University and a brace against Hawick. Overall the side chalked up sixteen victories in twenty games and achieved an aggregate score of 230 points to 117. With form like that it was hardly surprising that the national selectors were drawn to Goldenacre.

Neither was it a surprise when the still-uncapped Kinnear was selected for the British Lions tour to South Africa at the end of the next season. Until comparatively recently, the Lions had a strong tradition of selecting uncapped players. In the days before air travel, a Lions tour meant a long period of time away from home, for what were then amateur players.

Thus it was that distinguished players such as William Wavell Wakefield were unable or unwilling to make the 1924 tour, which was at least captained by a player of undisputed international class – England's Ronald Cove-Smith. Weakened by the exigencies of selection, and subjected to a savage run of injuries, the Lions did not perform well, securing only nine victories in twenty-nine games and losing the test series 3-0.

Despite being less than successful on the playing field, the tour left a prominent legacy. The team's ties sported a Lion motif and it was from this sartorial detail that the famous *Lions* name derived. Until that point the 'Lions'

SCOTLAND 1926
Scotland 0 - Ireland 3 - Edinburgh - 27th February 1926

D S Kerr   J C H Ireland   J Graham   W M Simmers   R M Kinnear   I S Smith
J C Dykes   H Waddell   J M Bannerman   D Drysdale (Captain)   D S Davies   D J MacMyn   J W Scott
J B Nelson   J R Paterson

had toured under a number of names (with 'The British Isles' probably being the most frequent and 'The English Rugby Football Team' the least politically correct, at least by today's standards). Political sensitivities continued, with the side being officially known as the British *and Irish* Lions since 2001 – but to most from 1924 onwards they have been, simply, *The Lions*.

The tour had personal legacies for Kinnear as well. Firstly, it brought him further to the attention of the Scottish selectors and, secondly, he will have noted the impact of injuries on many of his team mates. Players such as Thomas Holliday were sidelined for months as a result of playing an amateur game. For players with extensive private means this was not necessarily a problem. For those required to earn a living with their hands it was a serious matter, and had been one of the main reasons for the great split between union and league in 1895. Both Kinnear and Holliday would later go on to join the professional code.

Kinnear's Scotland debut came in 1926, away to France. The match took place on 2 January, presumably meaning a premature end to the players' traditional Hogmanay celebrations. The team showed no ill-effects from either the journey or the festivities, and secured a convincing 20-6 victory.

Kinnear retained his place for the next two home matches, with a narrow victory over Wales being followed by a disappointing 3-0 defeat to Ireland. The selectors were perhaps frustrated by Scotland's low scoring (Kinnear scored for neither the Lions nor Scotland) and he was left out for the next match in favour of Gordon Boyd in a rejigged back-line.

Kinnear's departure to join Wigan in the league was a major surprise and minor scandal. Scottish converts to the thirteen-a-side game tended to come from the Border clubs, who tended to have more players from working class backgrounds. Kinnear was a prominent representative of an Edinburgh public school side, usually seen as bastions of the establishment and the amateur game.

Whatever the reasons behind the move, Kinnear's talents as a rugby player made it a conspicuous success. He scored 81 tries in 182 games for the 'Cherry and Whites', including one against Dewsbury in a 1929 Challenge Cup Final victory, the first time the famous fixture was played at Wembley Stadium. He also played internationally on four occasions, once for England against Australia and three times for 'Other Nationalities'.

Having married his girlfriend Annie it was while living in Wigan that Roy's son, also called Roy, was born. The younger Roy would go on to become one of Britain's most famous character actors. Roy's son, Rory, has continued the family tradition and is himself a distinguished stage and television performer.

With the outbreak of war in 1939 the elder Roy joined the RAF and served as a flight sergeant. As in the First World War, the conflict saw a relaxing of the rules which normally forbade league players from competing in union matches. The 38-year-old Kinnear was playing for an RAF union team when he apparently collapsed and died from a heart attack.

The school's Roll of Honour remembers him simply but fondly as 'one of our greatest rugby players'.

Kinnear is commemorated in the Hillingdon and Uxbridge Cemetery, row O.D., grave 23.

Scotland

Lieutenant Commander Drummond St. Clair Ford
Scotland
Five tests
HM Submarine *Traveller*, Royal Navy
Died 12 December 1942, aged 34
Wing/centre

Pangbourne College.

Submariner presumed sunk off the Italian coast

Drummond St. Clair Ford was born on 16 December 1907 in Christchurch, Hants. He was the third and youngest son of six children born to Captain Anson St. Clair Ford and Isabel Maria Frances Adams. His eldest brother Aubrey would go on to inherit the St. Clair Ford baronetcy of Ember Court in Surrey. Drummond's surname is usually recorded as Ford in rugby sources.

His early years were spent in Christchurch, Hampshire. The town is an hour or so from Portsmouth, convenient for what was a long-established naval family, with all three sons continuing the tradition by serving as wartime commanders in the senior service.

Ford was educated at the Nautical College in Pangbourne. Located a surprisingly long distance from the sea, by the Thames in rural Berkshire, the college had been founded in 1917 with the intention of providing officers for both the Royal Navy and the merchant fleet. It was at school that Ford's rugby abilities first showed themselves. He and fellow future international H.C.C. Laird ensured the college's first XV was unbeaten in 1924, their final year at the school.

Ford joined the navy immediately on leaving Pangbourne, aged 17, and entered the submarine service in 1929. As with all naval officers, Ford's domestic and sporting life was interrupted by his service over- (or in his case under-) seas. Nevertheless, he frequently found time to play for both the Royal Navy and the United Services. At the time this was rugby of the highest quality. Ford was playing alongside greats like W.J.A. Davies, the winner of four Grand Slams for England (two as captain) and future internationals like J.W. Forrest.

He was selected to play for Scotland in 1930 by means of a slightly circuitous route. J.E. Hutton was initially chosen to make his debut at centre in the season's third match against Ireland, but apparently declined the invitation. Ford had played well in the season's two trials and was brought in, playing on the wing with W.M. Simmers moved to the centres to accommodate him.

NAUTICAL COLLEGE XV., 1924.

Played 15. Won 12. Drawn 1. Lost 2. Points 406–168.

Top Row (left to right): H. G. P. HARKER, W. A. F. HAWKINS, A. L. FRANKS, J. M. OLIVER, N. B RAMSAY, T. A. DAVIS, H. F. A. JACKSON, G. E. B. D. PAUL.
Bottom Row: C. E. A. OWEN, H. MORLAND, H. C. C. LAIRD, N. W. CULLUM, R. D. ST. C. FORD, H. DE M. MIDDLETON, J. J. OWEN.

The Irish match was played on 22 February, the visitors arriving on the back of two successive victories at Murrayfield. The weather was bitter, with braziers burning almost until kick-off to keep the frozen pitch just about playable. None of these factors worried Ford, who marked his debut with a try after just four minutes. According to *The Scotsman*, scrum half J.B. Nelson made a quick break and gave 'a long pass to Ford, who gathered the ball smartly and ran in strongly for a try'. Things nearly got even better for Ford, who made a scintillating break from his own 25-yard line to claim another try. Unfortunately this was, as *The Scotsman* put it, a 'prodigious waste of breath' as the referee had already blown for an infringement. The spectators, however, had enjoyed the excitement and cheered him all the way back down the pitch. The Scots eventually lost the match 14-11, with Ford coming close to rescuing at least a draw with a try at the end.

Despite this encouraging performance Ford was not initially selected for the season's next and final match – against England at Twickenham. However Ian Smith, Ford's partner on the wing for the Irish match, pulled out injured. Ford was in again, this time alongside the same J.E. Hutton who had declined the chance to play the Irish. Lining up against the Scots was Ford's United Services team mate, J.W. Forrest.

The English match was to end 0-0. Scoreless matches were not uncommon in rugby's very early days, but this would be one of only four such blank games for Scotland in the twentieth century. Ford does not appear to have been given too many chances to prove himself in the game and he must have been disappointed to be dropped for the first three matches of the 1931 season. He was recalled (at centre) for the match against England, and responded with a try in the only victory of his five-match international career. He played against Wales and Ireland in 1932, but lost on both occasions.

Ford married Miss Elizabeth Astley Maberley at St Paul's, Knightsbridge, in August 1933. They would have two sons and one daughter. With his domestic life settled and his international playing days behind him, Ford could concentrate on his naval career.

He was commissioned as an acting sub-lieutenant on 1 May 1928, became a sub-lieutenant on 1 January 1929 and lieutenant on 1 January 1931. By 1939 Ford had been promoted to lieutenant commander and would serve on submarines *H34, Sturgeon* and *Parthian*, seeing action in the North Sea, Atlantic and Mediterranean. He came to national attention in September 1940 when

SCOTLAND 1932

Scotland 0 - Wales 6 - Edinburgh - 6th February 1932

	M S Stewart	F H Waters	H S Mackintosh	D St C Ford	W R Logan	I S Smith
G Wood	J W Allan	W B Welsh	W M Simmers (Captain)	W N Roughead	J Beattie	J Graham
		H Lind		T H B Lawther		

SCOTLAND 1932
Scotland 8 - Ireland 20 - Edinburgh - 27th February 1932

F H Waters	M S Stewart	D St Clair Ford	W R Logan	A W Walker	I S Smith
J W Allan	R A Foster	W B Welsh	W M Simmers	H S Macintosh	J Beattie	G Wood
		W D Emslie	A H M Hutton		

he and his crew sunk a German transport ship off the Danish coast, with 'thousands' being reported drowned. In March 1941 he was again in the news, this time the success being an 8,000-tonne German tanker off Norway. These were vital morale boosters for the British public at desperate points in the war.

In November 1942 Ford was in command of his regular vessel, the *Parthian*, having recently completed their sixth voyage to resupply Malta and a short

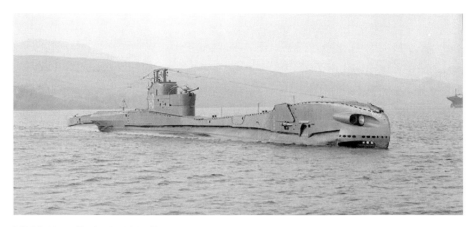

HMS *Traveller* in April 1942.

patrol off Sicily. Five tonnes of dehydrated cabbage and a large quantity of diesel fuel had been supplied to the besieged island, while the *Parthian* had suffered minor damage after being depth-charged twenty-one times by an Italian torpedo boat.

Ford was then given temporary command of the *Traveller*, replacing the submarine's usual skipper who had contracted dysentery.

Ford and the rest of the *Traveller's* crew left Malta on 28 November, urgently tasked with probing the defences around the Italian port of Taranto. The Royal Navy was preparing for Special Operation Principal, projected attacks on Italian ports by Chariot mini-submarines, also known as human torpedoes.

The *Traveller* did not respond to a signal sent on 8 December. She is assumed to have been destroyed by a mine in the Gulf of Taranto although her wreckage has never been found. Ford and his men are commemorated on the Portsmouth Naval Memorial, panel 61, column 3.

Lieutenant George Roberts
Scotland
Five tests
2nd Battalion, Gordon Highlanders
Died 2 August 1943, aged 29
Full Back

George Watson's
College.

Died on the Burma railway

George Roberts was born on 13 February 1914 in Edinburgh. He was the son of George and Jane Roberts. His education began at Mayfield Private School in Edinburgh, after which he attended George Watson's College in the city. Roberts' time at the college overlapped with two other boys who were also destined to play rugby for their country and to die in the Second World War: James McPhail Ritchie, who left the school in 1923, and A.S.B. McNeil who was in the year beneath Roberts.

On leaving the school Roberts promptly started to play for the Watsonians club, becoming the side's youngest ever captain and holding the position for five seasons. Roberts, Ritchie and McNeil would all play together for the ex-pupils club. They were also joined by Kenneth Roberts, George's younger brother and a fine scrum half and centre. Unlike the other three, Kenneth would not gain his cap, but he would go on to give his life in the war.

George worked for the National Bank of Scotland, which would become part of the Royal Bank of Scotland group. When not working or playing rugby it would appear that golf took up a fair amount of his time.

Roberts was a member of the Craigmillar Park Club, a short distance from the family home in Ladysmith Road. He was a sufficiently good player to be selected for his country, 1938 seeing him achieve what may well be a unique distinction – competing against all the other home nations in both rugby and golf.

Roberts was given his debut in the first match of the 1938 season, playing Wales at Murrayfield. 1937 had not been a good season for the Scots and the selectors had made swingeing changes to the team. Seven other debutants lined up with Roberts, two of whom – T.F. Dorward and J.G.S. Forrest – would also die in the war.

Scotland

The match was won 8-6. *The Scotsman* reported on the full back's performance with characteristic moderation: 'Roberts may never take place amongst the great Scottish full-backs but on Saturday he filled a difficult position with courage and real ability.' The newspaper sardonically reported a new-found consistency amongst the selectors with the headline, 'Once Despised XV chosen en bloc to meet Ireland'.

The match against Ireland was duly won, with a comprehensive 23-14 scoreline. *The Scotsman* was once again reserved, cautioning its readers not to get over-excited by the result and stating that Ireland were 'a very poor international side'.

The next match was against England at Twickenham. 'Wilson Shaw's Match' saw the Scottish skipper inspire his side to the Triple Crown with two magnificent tries. It is still seen by many as the finest-ever display by a Scottish back line (the forwards were well beaten, losing twenty-three of the twenty-seven second-half scrums).

Reporting the game, even the slightly dour *Scotsman* could only just avoid hyperbole. *The Aberdeen Press and Journal* was burdened by no such restraint, describing the 'Match of a Lifetime' and telling its readers how 'thrill followed thrill with bewildering rapidity'.

In common with all Scottish players, the 1939 season was a major disappointment for Roberts. The great Wilson Shaw was a shadow of his former self, and his players appeared to fade alongside him. Few performed well, and all three matches were lost. Roberts played against Wales and England, being forced to pull out of the Irish game through injury – his place being taken by W.M. Penman, who would also fall in the war. Clearly a valued member of the team, Roberts must have been disappointed to end his second season without scoring a point for his country.

The outbreak of the war saw Roberts join the 2nd Battalion, Gordon Highlanders. His brother Kenneth had joined the Royal Armoured Corps and was killed outside Dunkirk – dying the day after the evacuation ended.

Dunkirk was portrayed as a victory snatched from defeat. There could be no such illusion about the campaign that George was involved in. The Gordon Highlanders were stationed in Singapore when it was captured by the Japanese in what Churchill called 'the worst disaster and largest capitulation in British history'. Over 80,000 men were taken prisoner by a far smaller Japanese force.

The Japanese army's approach to both civilians and military personnel under its control was infamous in its brutality. Roberts was among the first 21,000 men held in the Selarang Barracks, designed for fewer than 1,000. From there they were marched to work on the Burmese railway – part of the Japanese plan to invade India.

Cruelty, disease and starvation rations led to a horrifyingly high death rate amongst the PoWs. Roberts succumbed on 2 August 1943.

Roberts is commemorated in Kanchanaburi war cemetery in Thailand, collective grave 6.G.1-67.

Wing Commander (Pilot) William Penman DFC AFC
Scotland
One test
61 Squadron RAF
Died 3 October 1943, aged 26
Full back

Flew with Guy Gibson VC

William Mitchell Penman was born in London on 12 May 1917. He was the son of George and Alice Penman. Although his family had a strong connection with London, where he was born, married and had his home at the time of his death, Penman came from a well-known Edinburgh sporting family.

He attended the city's Royal High School, reputedly the eighteenth oldest school in the world and, as might be expected of such a prominent Edinburgh school, a prolific provider of rugby talent. Twenty-six former pupils have been capped by Scotland, with four also captaining the national side. The suitably Scottish-sounding Angus Buchanan started the trend in 1871, helping to defeat the England XV and was later followed by the rather less stereotypically named Ivan Tukalo, who gained thirty-seven caps, including the memorable 1990 Grand Slam triumph over England at Murrayfield.

At the age of 18 Penman joined the RAF and received a commission as an acting pilot officer. He was also soon playing with distinction for the United Services, a traditional proving ground for would-be internationals from the army, navy and – more recently – the air force.

Despite his evident prowess, it seems unlikely that gaining international recognition would have been at the front of Penman's mind as the 1938/39 season began. As a serving RAF officer he must have been preoccupied with the deteriorating international situation, and in particular the menace being demonstrated by the Luftwaffe in the Spanish Civil War. In any case, Penman's position in the Scotland team, full-back, was occupied by George Roberts. Roberts had played with distinction in Scotland's Triple-Crown winning side of the previous season.

Scotland began the year with a match against Wales, fielding a very different side from Wilson-Shaw's triumphant team of the previous year. The captain was still present and Roberts was an automatic selection at full-back. These stalwarts shared the dressing room with a total of six new caps. Continuity did

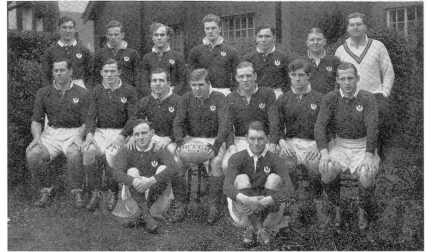

SCOTLAND 1939

Scotland 3 - Ireland 12 - Dublin - 25th February 1939

J R S Innes   R B Bruce Lockhart   I N Graham   D K A Mackenzie   I C Henderson   W Purdie   C H Gadney (Referee)
A Roy   D J Macrae   K C Fyfe   R W Shaw (Captain)   G B Horsburgh   W B Young   G D Shaw
T F Dorward   W M Penman

not seem to be high on the list of priorities. Perhaps unsurprisingly, the team responded with a dreadful performance and Wales won 11-3.

For the match against Ireland the selectors responded in predictable fashion, making eight changes. Initially Penman was not named in the squad. However at the last minute both Roberts and the nominated reserve, C.F. Grieve, reported themselves as injured. Penman was drafted in, to a distinctly muted welcome from the Scottish press. *The Aberdeen Journal*, for example, referred to him as one of the selectors' 'periodic unknowns' and noted that he had played without any 'particular distinction' in a pre-trial match.

Whatever the views of the newspapers, Penman was in the team for the match, played at Lansdowne Road on 25 February. The game was dominated by the foul weather, a waterlogged pitch and a set of rampaging Irish loose forwards. Forward 'rushes', dribbling and hacking the ball forward, were still a prominent feature of play at this time, and were perfectly suited to the appalling weather conditions. The Irish exploited them to the full and won 12-3. When the Scots did manage to secure possession, they were constantly harassed and pressurized into making mistakes.

The Scotsman summarized: 'WM Penman, who had an extremely severe debut, did about as much as can be expected.' Although this must have felt like being damned with faint praise, it was at least better than the tone of reporting which had welcomed his selection. Bill could reflect on a job reasonably well done, but can hardly have been surprised when Roberts was recalled for the English match.

In December of 1939 Penman was engaged to the glamorous Miss Peggy MacCorkindale, a Scottish junior lawn tennis champion and future Wimbledon quarter-finalist. The ceremony took place at Hendon on the eighth of January 1940, earlier than expected due to news of Penman's posting overseas. Bill's brother David was able to take leave from his duties as a fellow RAF pilot and serve as best man. The shortage of time meant that many of the eighty guests were summoned by telephone. Penman's mother arrived by train from Edinburgh but his father's wartime duties kept him in Edinburgh. Such were the exigencies of wartime life.

Penman's overseas posting was to Camp Borden in Ontario, Canada, which had been the birthplace of the Royal Canadian Air Force in 1917. By the time Penman arrived, in January 1940, it was a key hub in the British Commonwealth Air Training Plan, of which Penman was to be second-in-command. Put simply, British airbases were too busy, too short of fuel, too vulnerable to attack and too badly affected by inclement weather to serve as effective training bases. The RAF neatly solved the problem by outsourcing the training to Canada, with its wide-open spaces, ample fuel and location between the European and Pacific theatres of war. While there, Penman was decorated with the Air Force Cross (AFC) in recognition of his valuable services to flying instruction while attached to the RCAF.

He returned to Britain in October 1942 and was posted to a Lancaster squadron. In February 1943, after undergoing some operational training himself, the former instructor arrived at RAF Syerston as CO of 61 Squadron. Wing Commander Penman and his crews shared the Nottinghamshire base with 106 Squadron, led by Guy Gibson VC of Dambusters fame. In fact Penman went on several raids with Gibson, one of which is described below:

Another Lancaster squadron [61] from this station which bombed Essen last night is commanded by Wing Commander W. M. Penman, A.F.C. He and Wing Commander Gibson led their squadrons together in the big raid on Cologne. It was a 'wizard prang'. When the last of his crews had returned from Essen and completed their interrogation Wing Commander Penman left here for London to captain the RAF Rugger XV in the match against Combined Universities. After the game he is entering hospital to undergo an operation for appendicitis.

Penman was decorated with the DFC for completing two missions regardless of the fact that his gun turrets had failed. On another occasion an engine failed but despite this he successfully bombed the target and brought his aircraft and crew home safely.

Penman had been quick to pick up his rugby career on returning from Canada and continued to play despite operational sorties and his responsibilities as CO. On 25 September 1943 he was captaining the RAF against a South Wales side. Over 4,000 people were drawn to the match – perhaps not surprising given the paucity of wartime entertainment and the fact that the RAF team alone contained thirteen internationals.

Just over a week after the match in Swansea, on the night of 3/4 October 1943, Penman took off for the last time. Fifteen planes left Syerston targeting Kassel in central Germany. Penman was piloting W4279 QR-Z 'Zebra', one of three of the planes which did not return. It was later reported: 'All personnel at 61 Squadron were devastated when they got the news that their Commanding Officer had been lost in action during the night operation to Kassel on the 3/4th October 1943. The sense of shock was exacerbated by the fact that he and his highly experienced crew were considered to be "indestructible".' Penman was killed along with all his crew, which consisted of:

P/O. K.J. Stephenson (flight engineer)
F/L E.W. Mitchell (navigator)
F/L D.L. Thomson (bomb aimer)
F/L D.I. Wilkinson (W/T operator, air gunner)
F/O M.R. Braines (air gunner 1)
P/O Maurice Root-Reed (air gunner 2)

Penman had only just been told of his promotion to acting group captain and was due to take up the rank the following day. He left behind his wife, Peggy, and their ten-month old daughter Susan. Susan later served as the 61 Squadron Associations' dining secretary. Penman is commemorated in the Hanover War Cemetery, memorial reference 3.A.8.

Major George Gallie MC
Scotland
One test
78 Field Regiment, Royal Artillery
Died 16 January 1944, aged 26
Prop

'And all the brothers were valiant'

George Holmes Gallie was born on 17 September 1917 in Edinburgh. His father, Robert Arthur Gallie, played eight times as hooker for Scotland in 1920-1. His international career followed closely after distinguished service in the First World War.

Robert Gallie also played in the 1919 King's Cup, a tournament organised amongst teams from the allied armies after the 1918 armistice. Because of its high standard and international composition the tournament is often regarded as a precursor of the rugby World Cup, which did not make its debut until 1987. Gallie played in all six matches contested by the 'mother country', including the final in which the British side (minus the RAF, who played separately) lost to the New Zealand Army.

George was the eldest of Robert's three sons, all of whom would serve in the Second World War. The middle son, Robert Eric, was killed at Bruyelle in Belgium in the German offensive of May 1940. Alexander Knox, the youngest son, was fighting in Italy when George was killed nearly four years later. He was withdrawn from the front line in order to save his family any further suffering, but one imagines the trauma can only have contributed to Robert's death at the age of only 55 in 1948.

George began his schooling at Edinburgh Academy after which, like his father and brothers, he attended Fettes College in the city. He completed his education at Edinburgh University, taking a degree in law and graduating in 1939. By the same year his performances as a loose forward for Edinburgh Academicals had brought him to the attention of the Scottish selectors.

1938 had ended gloriously for Scotland. Captain Wilson Shaw and the rest of his back line had mesmerised England while securing the Triple Crown at Twickenham. The selectors' problem, however, was that the backs had been playing behind a comprehensively beaten pack. They knew that they needed to find a solution to the problem, especially in the front row.

Apparently deciding that drastic situations called for drastic solutions, the selectors chose an entirely new front row for the first match of the 1939 season, away to Wales. Gallie played at prop, with Sampson hooking between him and fellow prop Purdie. The selectors' move was especially bold given that Gallie turned out for his club in the back row.

The match was played on 4 February and was to prove the last international to be played in Cardiff for eight years. The selectors' gamble failed to pay off, with Scotland soundly beaten 11-3 by Wilf Wooler's Welsh team. In truth the pack's performance was adequate, and the loss was more down to a lacklustre

Gallie can be seen on the back row, third from the right.

display by Wilson Shaw, who had been 'indisposed' on the journey to Cardiff. The Scottish captain was in indifferent form all season and his team suffered as a result. Scotland would lose all three games of the season and enter the war as wooden spoon holders.

Gallie's personal performance appears to have been competent but unremarkable. He features little in the match reports, with *The Scotsman* stating merely that he was 'somewhat subdued except for one grand saving tackle' – apparently retaining his back row versatility even when packing with the tight five. He and Sampson were dropped for the next match against Ireland with Purdie surviving to play twice more.

As might be expected of sons of such a distinguished soldier, George and his brothers served in the Officer Training Corps and the Territorial Army. In George's case he was commissioned in the 78th (Lowland) Field Regiment, part of the Royal Artillery, in 1936 before being promoted to captain with the outbreak of war.

The 78th served in North Africa where artillery played a crucial role in Field Marshal Montgomery's decisive victory over Rommel's Afrika Korps at El Alamein. Gallie and the regiment's 24 pounders were heavily involved. After El Alamein Gallie saw further action in the Middle East. He was promoted to major and awarded the Military Cross for distinguished service.

The 78th were involved in the invasion of Sicily in 1943 and the subsequent campaign to occupy mainland Italy. Another young Scottish rugby player was serving with the artillery in this campaign. In Bill McLaren's case he was acting as an advanced artillery spotter. Tuberculosis would rob McLaren of the chance to follow Gallie into the Scottish side, but would not prevent him from developing his career as a peerless television commentator.

Gallie was killed when crossing the River Garigliano on 16 January 1944, the very outbreak of the long battle for control of Monte Cassino. The hilltop monastery was the lynchpin of the German line defending Rome. This natural strongpoint was reduced to ruins by concentrated bombing and artillery fire. The ruins provided perfect defensive positions for the German troops and it would take five months of hard fighting to remove them. Gallie was one of an estimated 55,000 Allied casualties.

He is commemorated in the Minturno War Cemetery in Italy, grave reference III, B, 18.

Surgeon Lieutenant Alastair McNeil
Scotland
One test
HMS *LST-422*, Royal Naval Volunteer Reserve
Died 26 January 1944, aged 28
Prop

George Watson's
College.

Killed during the Anzio landings

Alastair Simpson Bell McNeil was born on 28 January 1915 in Edinburgh. He was educated at George Watson's College in Edinburgh, where he captained both the cricket and rugby teams. His prowess on the rugby field was recognized by selection for the Scottish Public Schools in their match against their English equivalents. He left Watson's to study medicine at Edinburgh University.

It was while at university that McNeil gained his one international rugby cap, away to Ireland on 23 February 1935. McNeil was playing as a forward

SCOTLAND 1935

Scotland 5 - Ireland 12 - Edinburgh - 23rd February 1935

D A Thom	W G S Johnston	W A Burnet	G S Cottington	A S B M'Neil	K W Marshall
R M Grieve	W R Logan	J Beattie	R W Shaw (Captain)	J A Waters	R C S Dick	L B Lambie
		K C Fyfe		H Lind	

(positions were less specialized in that era) for the Watsonians club. He was not initially selected for the match and the Scottish team travelled to Dublin without him. At the last minute, however, the prop Roy Murray was injured. The selectors decided to call for McNeil from Edinburgh, despite having several travelling replacements in Ireland. Scotland had lost the season's first match, away to Wales. They were hoping to get their season back on track with a victory in Dublin – described as 'the capital of the Free State' by the newspaper correspondents, for whom Irish independence was still apparently a novel phenomenon.

Ireland denied the Scots their victory with a strong performance on a typically wet and windy February afternoon. The Scots had real talent in their backline, as shown in their spectacular first-half try which saw Wilson Shaw sprint in after a wonderful break from Charles Dick. Generally, however, the ball was too greasy to suit this sort of play and the Scots could not match the strength or endeavour of the Irish pack.

The final score was 12-5 to Ireland. The *Dundee Evening Telegraph* headlined its report 'Our Forwards Flopped – And the Game Was Lost'. The newspaper acknowledged that McNeil had worked hard, but also observed that 'the young Watsonian is on the light side'. Perhaps agreeing that the side needed more heft, the selectors recalled Murray for the final game – a home victory against England. The Scots finished bottom of the table, which was topped by Ireland with two victories. McNeil had played his one and only game for Scotland.

Playing alongside McNeil in Dublin was W.R. Logan. A fellow student at Edinburgh University, Logan would play twenty times for Scotland. At the time of the Dublin match Logan was already a dual international, his one cricket cap having come against a touring South American side in 1932, whereas McNeil had to wait two more years for international cricket recognition.

On 11 and 12 August 1937 McNeil turned out to play cricket for Scotland against Yorkshire at Harrogate. Included in the Yorkshire side was the great Len Hutton, fresh from scoring his maiden test century against New Zealand and at the start of a test career that would last until 1955. McNeil was an all-rounder, combining his batting with slow left-arm bowling but – given the level of opposition – was perhaps relieved not to be asked to bowl during the match.

The game did not go well for the Scots. After winning the toss Yorkshire decided to bat and scored 291, with Hutton contributing 45. Neither of the Scottish openers bothered the scorers and, when McNeil was caught out for five, the score was eleven for five. All out for 104 in the first innings, the Scots managed to reach 143 in the second with McNeil bagging a respectable 23 before being run out. All-in-all, an easy innings victory for Yorkshire and not much excitement for the 3,000 spectators. McNeil played cricket twice more for Scotland, but this was his only first-class game.

McNeil graduated from Edinburgh in 1938, and his career in first-class sport came to an end as he developed his medical career with spells in Worthing and Ventnor.

With the outbreak of war he served with the Royal Naval Volunteer Reserve, seeing action in Madagascar, North Africa and Italy.

On 26 January 1944 McNeil was embarked upon *LST-422*, a tank landing craft bound for the Anzio bridgehead. The landings at Anzio were designed to bypass the strong German defences which were holding up the Allied advance towards Rome. The expedition's failure is often put down to timidity on the part of General Lucas, the commanding officer, but in reality he was hamstrung by a lack of materials and the ships to deliver them. Landing craft like the one in which McNeil was travelling were being enviously guarded for the forthcoming invasion of France, and precious few were available for the Anzio landings. McNeil was in a convoy of fourteen ships, carrying crucial supplies for the troops already ashore, when *422* struck a mine in appalling weather. Over 400 men were lost and McNeil was last seen 'ignoring his own safety in an attempt to save the lives of other people'.

His body was never recovered and McNeil is commemorated on the Chatham Naval Memorial (panel 79.3) and at his school.

Scotland

Captain William Renwick
Scotland
Two tests
1 Regiment, Royal Horse Artillery
Died 15 June 1944, aged 29
Wing

Killed while commanding his battery

William Norman Renwick was born on 29 November 1914 in Edinburgh. Renwick's parents, William Barr and Helen Nora Renwick, lived in Edinburgh, but the family also had connections in Kushtia, in what is now Bangladesh but was then Bengal. Renwick attended Loretto School in Edinburgh where his sporting and academic prowess led him to become head boy.

Loretto enjoyed a prestigious rugby fixture list and Renwick played against far-flung sides such as Sedbergh School in Cumbria as well as closer-to-home rivals such as Fettes. A centre, his promise was recognised early and he was selected to play for the Scottish Public Schools against their English counterparts at Richmond on New Year's Day, 1935.

University College Oxford provided the next stage in Renwick's rugby development. Amongst his contemporaries at the university was *the* dazzling star of the rugby scene at the time – Prince Alexander Obolensky, a White Russian émigré, and winger of extraordinary speed and verve. By January 1936 Obolensky had announced himself to the wider world with two stunning tries for England against the touring All Blacks, caught for posterity by the Pathé News cameras. There had been a few mutterings about the propriety of a Russian playing for England, but these tended to go away in the aftermath of England's first victory over New Zealand. The game is still known as Obolensky's match, and his tries are no less magical when viewed on YouTube.

Obolensky's was a flame that burned brightly but not for long. He enjoyed a lavish lifestyle – champagne and oysters were often on his pre-match menu (though many thought his rugby career suffered as a result). He played in all of England's 1936 internationals but injury and erratic form meant he would never feature again.

Obolensky's chance to confound his detractors, and secure selection, came in the following season's Varsity match. The Oxford versus Cambridge match was then a game of the highest quality, an unofficial international trial which gained worldwide coverage. Unfortunately for Obolensky, he was injured in the run-up to the game. Renwick was playing as a centre for his college, but his speed and class meant that he was an obvious replacement for the star international winger.

As he would do often during his career, Renwick confirmed the wisdom of his selection with an early try. On this occasion it was not enough to deny Cambridge victory, but Renwick would get his chance the following year. The Varsity match of December 1937 was stuffed with past and future internationals (Obolensky included) and attracted George VI to Twickenham for the first visit of his reign. He was rewarded with a cracker of a game, with Renwick again crossing early as unfancied Oxford outscored Cambridge by five tries to nil.

The match's profile was so high it is no surprise to find extensive coverage in the *Townsville Daily News*. Townsville may be in Queensland, Australia, and 10,000 miles from Twickenham but in 1937 its readers were kept well informed:

> *Play passed bewilderingly from end to end in quick sequence, and at breakneck speed and [the] excitement was almost too much for some of the Old Brigade in the stands.*

Renwick's performance was not quite good enough to earn selection for Scotland's first game of the 1938 season, a victory at home to Wales, or the following game, another Murrayfield victory, over the Irish. However, for the final game of the season, against England at Twickenham with a Triple Crown to be won, the selectors had a problem. On England's wing was Hal Sever, who had partnered Obolensky on the wing against the All Blacks and also scored a try. More consistent than the Russian, Sever had gone on to score vital points in every one of England's Triple Crown victories of the 1937 season. The Scottish selectors did not trust the incumbent Archibald Drummond to match Sever's pace and so turned to Renwick to nullify the threat.

True to form, Renwick justified the selectors' faith with an early try. He later added another as Wilson Shaw inspired Scotland's backline to five tries. England could muster only one try in response, Scotland won a famous victory, and Renwick was judged to have done a good job in keeping Sever quiet. King George was again in attendance and was by now presumably looking for Renwick's name on the team sheet.

Renwick can be seen here in this New Zealand team photo on the back row, third from the left.

Many people thought Renwick fortunate to have been selected for the first game of the following season, away to Wales. He had been playing indifferently for his club side, and this form continued into the international arena. He made no glaring errors, but was anonymous in attack and was one of the players who paid the price for a poor team performance. Scotland were defeated 11-3 and Renwick was not to play for Scotland again.

Renwick joined the artillery with the outbreak of war in 1939. He worked his way through the ranks, receiving a commission and joined Chestnut Troop 1st Regiment RHA. He served in the Middle East and North Africa. He fought through the battle of Alamein and the subsequent pursuit of Rommel's army. After being promoted captain he accompanied the regiment to Italy in the spring of 1944. The artillery were much in demand as allied forces battered their way through successive lines of well-prepared German defences. He was killed in action on 15 June 1944 while acting as commander of No. 1 Battery, near Bolsena, about seventy miles north of Rome. He is commemorated in the Bolsena War Cemetery, grave reference I.D.14.

Eric Liddell
Scotland
Seven tests
Civilian casualty
Died 21 February 1945, aged 43
Winger

They shall mount up with wings as eagles;
they shall run and not be weary.
(Isaiah 40:31 – made famous in the Film Chariots of Fire*)*

Rugby Football and the concept of Muscular Christianity developed hand-in-hand at Rugby School in Warwickshire in the early nineteenth century. One century later, Eric Henry Liddell would emerge as the very epitome of the ideal envisaged by Rugby's headmaster Thomas Arnold.

Muscular Christianity championed sport and competition as ways of preparing fit, devout and competent leaders for service in the British Empire. Rugby was viewed as the ideal means to put the theory into action.

Muscular activities were important to Liddell, but there can be no doubt that Christianity was the defining factor in his life. It was his faith that would lead to his refusal to run in the 100 metres at the 1924 Paris Olympics. This refusal is at the heart of the Oscar-winning film *Chariots of Fire* and is what Liddell is best known for, but he was also a star rugby player who won seven caps for his country while still at university.

Liddell was born on 16 January 1902 in Tientsin, China. He was the second son of the Reverend and Mrs James Dunlop Liddell, Scottish missionaries with the London Missionary Society. Liddell went to school in China until the age of 5. At the age of 6, he and his 8-year-old brother Robert were enrolled in Eltham College, a boarding school in south London for the sons of missionaries. Their parents and

sister Jenny then returned to China. During the boys' time at Eltham, their parents, sister Jenny, and new brother Ernest came home on furlough two or three times and were able to be together as a family, mainly living in Edinburgh.

Liddell studied pure science at Edinburgh University between 1920 and 1924, combining his studies with sporting activities and conspicuous religious devotion in a way which would have made Arnold proud.

In rugby terms, his raw pace alone would have made him a natural on the wing but, as *The Student* confirmed in June 1922, he had far more to offer rugby than merely speed:

EH Liddell has the rare combination of pace and the gift of rugby brains and hands. Makes openings, snaps opportunities, gives the 'dummy' to perfection, does the work of three if necessary, in defence, and carries unselfishness to a fault.

International recognition for Liddell's rugby talents came in 1922. He made his debut at Stade Colombes in a disappointing 3-3 draw with France on 2 January, following that up with another draw, 9-9 at home to Wales. His first victory and try both arrived in the next match, 6-3 at home to Ireland. He picked up a leg injury in a friendly game and had to withdraw from the last match of the season, away to England.

Scotland enjoyed a more successful season in 1923, remaining unbeaten until their final match against England at Inverleith. Liddell had scored a try in each of the three preceding victories against France, Wales and Ireland. Unfortunately the Scots came up against a truly great England side, led by 'Dave' Davies and including such players as Wavell Wakefield and Cyril Lowe. England won 8-6, and went on to win the Grand Slam – a feat they would repeat the following season. The match marked the end of Liddell's international career, as he retired from the game to concentrate on his preparations for the 1924 Games.

By a strange quirk of fate the athletics events were to be held in the same Stade Colombes where Liddell had made his rugby debut. Contrary to the portrayal in *Chariots of Fire*, Liddell knew months in advance that the stadium would hold the heats of his favourite event, the 100 metres, on a Sunday. His faith left him no option but to concentrate on the 200 and 400 metre races.

Like many great films, *Chariots of Fire* takes the occasional liberty with the truth. It is, however, almost painfully accurate in its portrayal of the emotion surrounding Liddell's victory in the 400. Liddell was already a man famous for pushing himself to, and occasionally beyond, the limits of endurance in pursuit of victory. No spectator could remain unmoved as he, with that characteristic head-back running style, sprinted the first half of the race flat out and then used all his physical and spiritual strength to hold on for victory down the home straight.

Liddell's triumph in the 400 came a few days after he had won bronze in the 200 metres, beating Harold Abraham (played by Ben Cross in the film) into sixth place. Liddell returned to Edinburgh to graduate. After the ceremony his fellow students showed their admiration by carrying him in triumph through the streets of Edinburgh.

Less than a year later Liddell was back in Tientsin, following in his parents' missionary footsteps. His humility and decency continued to inspire and impress almost everyone he met. In 1934 he married Canadian Florence Mackenzie, with whom he would have three daughters.

With the 1937 Japanese invasion of China, life in the country became increasingly dangerous. Florence and the girls returned to Canada but Eric stayed with his ministry. In 1943 he was interned in Weixien camp, where he defied the harsh conditions to lead, nurture and care for other inmates. The conditions and his relentless efforts for others took their toll. In his last letter home, written the day before he died, Liddell wrote of suffering a nervous breakdown due to overwork. In fact he had an inoperable brain tumour. He died on 21 February 1945, five months before liberation. Liddell's last words were, 'It's complete surrender'.

A fellow inmate of the camp, Langdon Gilkey, wrote,

Scotland

He was overflowing with good humour and love for life, and with enthusiasm and charm. It is rare indeed that a person has the good fortune to meet a saint, but he came as close to it as anyone I have ever known.

The Scotsman ended its tribute by quoting from Frances Harvegal's famous hymn *Take my Life and Let It Be*:

Take my feet and let them be
Swift and beautiful for thee.

Liddell was buried in the garden behind the Japanese officers' quarters in what is now Weifeng Middle School in Shandong Province, his grave marked by a small wooden cross. The site was forgotten until it was rediscovered in 1989 due to the hard work of an engineer by the name of Charles Walker who was working in Hong Kong. In 1991 Edinburgh University erected a memorial headstone, made from Isle of Mull granite at the former camp site in Weifeng. The inscription carved onto the stone said, 'They shall mount up with wings as eagles; they shall run and not be weary.'

Wales

**Squadron Leader Cecil Rhys Davies
Mentioned in Despatches
Welsh
One test
224 Squadron Royal Air Force Volunteer Reserve
Died 24 December 1941, aged 32
Prop**

The First BOAC pilot to die in the war

Cecil Rhys Davies was born on 12 September 1909 in Pontypridd, Wales. He was the son of William Rhys Davies and Elizabeth Anne of Monmouthshire. He was educated at Cardiff High School where he first learned his rugby skills and his talent for the game was quickly spotted. He won two Welsh Secondary Schools caps in 1926, going on to play for Cardiff, London Welsh and Bedford.

Deciding on a career with the RAF he took a short-term commission as a Pilot Officer on probation in 1934 (*London Gazette* 13 March 1931). While with the RAF he continued with his sports, becoming the RAF heavyweight boxing

WALES 1934
Wales 0 - England 9 - Cardiff - 20th January 1934

H Packer (Touch Judge)   A M Rees   C R Davies   Gome Hughes   H Trueman   D Thomas   Ken Jones   F Haslett (Referee)
Lieut. B T V Cowey   B Howells   C Davey   J R Evans (Captain)   J I Rees   G Rees Jones   Glyn Prosser
C W Jones   D D Evans

champion. He also played rugby for the RAF, representing them in the inter-services tournament of 1933 and 1934. In August 1934 however he left the RAF and began training as a pilot with BOAC.

Taking a commission with the RAF at the outbreak of the Second World War, he was promoted from flight lieutenant to squadron leader on 10 June 1941. He served with 224 Squadron Coastal Command, flying Lockheed Hudsons. 224 was a Coastal Command squadron that began the war as a maritime reconnaissance squadron. The squadron became operational in August, moving to its first wartime base at Leuchars in Scotland, flying patrols over the North Sea looking for German shipping as well as providing air cover for convoys. On 8 October a Hudson from the squadron reported sighting a German force consisting of a battleship, a cruiser and four destroyers off the south-west coast of Norway, although bad weather prevented the sighting from being followed up.

Anti-shipping operations were added to the squadron's duties after the German invasion of Norway. In April 1941 the squadron moved to Northern Ireland to fly anti-submarine patrols. In December it moved to Cornwall to fly patrols off Brest as well as attack shipping off Brittany.

The squadron flew out of St Eval in Cornwall. In fact they demolished the village of St Eval in order to build the Coastal Command station. Only the church was left and that was used as the squadron church. It is still there.

Davies, flying his Lockheed Hudson Mark V serial number AM669 marking QX-F, was sent out on a patrol. The aircraft failed to return. Despite searches it was never seen again. Weather conditions, enemy action or mechanical problems – no one was ever sure why it came down. The crew were made up of Squadron Leader Cecil Rhys Davies, Flight Lieutenant Joseph Herbert Higgleton, Sergeant Arthur George Gooch and Sergeant Jack Roberts.

Squadron Leader Davies' body was later washed up in France and he is buried in the Bayeux War Cemetery in France, plot VIII.C.21. The other members of his crew are listed on the Runnymede Memorial.

Lieutenant John Evans
Wales
One test
3 Parachute Regiment, Army Air Corps
Died 8 March 1943, aged 31
Hooker

'I would miss him – the naughty glint in his eye when he recalled an escapade following an International rugby match. Thoughts lingered for many days until my initial sadness was dispelled'

John Raymond Evans was born on 12 September 1911 in Newport, Wales. He was the son of William John and Alice Evans. He was educated at the Newport High School where he first learned to pick up a ball and run with it, making the school's first XV. He actually won three caps for Newport RFC while still a school boy, playing as a hooker, having shown his mettle as a Welsh school boy. On leaving school he became a bank clerk for Lloyds Bank at Newport and Chesham and worked in the offices of the accountants Messrs Walter Hunter, Bartlett Thomas and Company.

He also began playing his rugby for Chiltern RFC (1929/30) at the well-known Pineapple ground. Chiltern was a much smaller club than Newport with far fewer supporters. He was a resounding success, scoring over fifty points in his first three games despite being played out of position for the first few. He eventually returned to Newport in February 1930, but only managed five first class games before the end of the season. After that however he was a regular player for Newport, making no fewer than a 150 first class appearances for the club before 1938. He captained the side for two seasons in 1935-37. On 31 October 1935 he captained Newport against the visiting New Zealanders at Rodney Parade, Newport. Newport lost by seventeen points to five. He was also a member of the unbeaten Barbarians' Easter tour of 1935.

His fine form came to the notice of the Welsh selectors and he was selected to play for Wales during the Home Nations against England on 20 January 1934 at the National Stadium, Cardiff. Interestingly he was one of only four Welsh Internationals ever to captain the side on his debut game. Evans later said the only reason for this was that he was the only player in either side that spoke both Welsh and English. He was also one of thirteen new caps to play in the game that day. Unfortunately Wales was well beaten zero points to nine. The selectors were later severely criticized for their choice, not only because of the teams' inexperience, but also because seven of the team played their rugby outside Wales. It was to be Evans only international match.

With his rugby career coming to an end, Evans moved to the Gold Coast of Africa and worked for the Forestry Commission for almost three years.

With the outbreak of the war, Evans returned to the UK and took an emergency commission into the South Wales Borderers in March 1941. Keen to see action Evans joined 7 Platoon, C Company of the 3rd Parachute Battalion. Hundreds of men volunteered to join the new airborne forces and few were selected. However Evans was almost certainly helped with his application by Major Alan Bush (company commander in the 3rd Para Battalion). Bush was a former Oxford rugby blue who had played against Evans in a Major Stanley's XV.

The 3rd Battalion was formed in September 1941 at Hardwick in Derbyshire by its first commander Lieutenant Colonel G.W. Lathbury. From an initial 500 volunteers only 100 were selected for training. Intense parachute training then took place at RAF Ringway throughout the autumn of 1941 with many dropping out through injury and unsuitability. By 1942 the battalion were ready to get on with the war. Its first action was the capture of the German airfield at Bône in Tunisia, on 12 November 1942. It was the first British army battalion level parachute operation. After this operation the battalion fought with the infantry for the remainder of the North African campaign, retaining their battle cry of 'Waho Mohammed' which had been picked up in Africa and became popular across the regiment and brigade.

Lieutenant Evans was shot and killed by a German sniper on the morning of 8 March 1943 with a single shot to the head while defending a crossroads during preliminary skirmishes around Sedjenane shortly before the Battle of Tamera in Tunisia. He was still smoking his familiar pipe. Major Bush later recalled,

It was when we reached the defensive position that I saw the dead. The injuries to our dead were gruesome, and at the time it was the general opinion that the attackers had used Dum Dum bullets. In a fleeting moment my immediate thoughts were that I remembered John's acceptance of the orders I had reluctantly given to him, the most horrible job I have ever ordered. He had received them as a challenge with a spirited glint in his eye, a visible reluctance, as much to say 'If you insist'. He had not been the best of Regimental officers, for in him was too much of the rebel, too much individuality in his great body for that, yet some instinct made him always respond rightly and immediately to the needs of the occasion. I would miss him – the naughty glint in his eye when he recalled an escapade following an International rugby match. Thoughts lingered for many days until my initial sadness was dispelled.

Jocky Allen, Evans's batman, also remembered him,

He was not the typical officer. On route marches he would sing 'We will keep the red flag flying high' and would turn up at the pub and have drinking contests with members of his platoon – no one could beat him. His platoon would follow him anywhere and did so when action was called for.

The sniper that killed John Evans was later wounded and captured wearing two red cross bands. He was lucky not to get shot on the spot. He was loaded into an ambulance and driven to a field hospital, and en route the ambulance was hit by a German shell and everyone in it was burned to death.

John was initially buried close to where he fell like so many of his comrades. However his remains were later removed and he is now buried in the Tabarka Ras Rajel war cemetery, Tunisia, grave reference 4.E.8., surrounded by his former comrades. The inscription on his CWGC headstone reads,

In Loving Memory of Our Darling John
"Until we meet again"
Mother and Bunny

Wales

Major Maurice Turnbull
Wales
Two tests
First Battalion the Welsh Guards
Died 5 August 1944, aged 38
Scrum half

The only man to play cricket for England and rugby for Wales

Maurice Joseph Lawson Turnbull was born on 16 March 1906 in Cardiff, the son of Philip Bernard (1879-1930), ship owner, and Annie Marie Hennessy Oates Turnbull (1879-1942). He was almost destined to have a sporting career. His father was a Welsh international hockey player taking a bronze medal at the 1908 Olympic games held in London. Six of his eight sons also played for Cardiff Rugby Club.

Turnbull was educated at Downside (the sixth form bar is still named after him) where he played cricket for the first XI and rugby for the first XV. On leaving school he went up to Trinity College Cambridge. He got his blue for hockey and cricket and like so many people who play sports to a very high level he excelled at many other sports too. He played hockey for both his University and Wales, rackets for his university, and squash for Wales being a founder member of the

PLAYER'S CIGARETTES

M J. TURNBULL (GLAMORGAN)

Cardiff Squash Rackets Club and winning the squash rackets championship of South Wales. He played rugby for St Peters, Cardiff, Glamorgan, Cambridge University, London Welsh and Somerset.

Turnbull was selected to play for Wales twice, both during the Home Nations championship (his elder brother, Bernard, had already represented Wales). He made his debut against England at Twickenham on 21 January 1933, being one of seven fresh caps brought into the Welsh side. Wales won the game 3-7 breaking the so-called 'Twickenham Bogey' (ten losses in ten visits). Ronnie Boon downed a try and kicked a drop goal for Wales.

Turnbull was unable to play against Scotland due to an injury but was selected once again to play against Ireland at Ravenhill, Belfast, on 11 March 1933. This time Wales went down 10-5, Harry Bowcott downing a try and Viv Jenkins kicking the conversion. It was to be Turnbull's last game for Wales.

On 7 September 1939 Turnbull married Elizabeth Brooke, the only daughter of William Brooke of Scunthorpe, Lincs. They had three children: Sara, Simon and Georgina.

During the war Turnbull was commissioned into the Welsh Guards rising to the rank of major. He was killed in action while commanding No.2 Company 1st Battalion by a sniper's bullet shortly after the Normandy Landings on 5 August 1944 during the fighting for the French village of Montchamp. His body was lost for a while, but Sergeant Frederick Llewellyn searched the battlefield, at no small risk to himself, and found Turnbull's remains. His personal possessions were later sent home to his family.

Turnbull is buried in Bayeux War Cemetery, grave reference XX.C.3. Well worth a visit and a few flowers.

Turnbull also played cricket for England, playing in nine tests. He also made 388 first class appearances for Cambridge University, Glamorgan and Wales. He is the only person to have played cricket for England and rugby for Wales.

Turnbull wrote two cricketing books with fellow international Maurice Allom, *The Book of Two Maurices* (1930) and *The Two Maurices Again* (1931). The books gave accounts of their cricket tours to New Zealand and South Africa.

Appendix One

Losses in date order

Prince Alexander Sergeevich Obolensky, England, 29-3-40
Emile Doussau, France, 28-4-40
Paul Cooke, England, 28-5-40
François Meret, France, 10-6-40
Donald Kenneth Andrew Mackenzie, Scotland, 12-6-40
Bryan (Brian) Henry Black, England, 29-7-40
Donald Gordon Cobden, New Zealand, 11-8-40
Ernest Ian Parsons, England, 14-8-40
Derek Edmund Teden, England, 15-10-40
Henry Rew, England, 11-12-40
George Ernest Luddington, England, 10-1-41
Thomas Dorward, Scotland, 5-3-41
Charles Francis George Thomas Hallaran, Ireland, 21-3-41
Patric Bernard Coote, Ireland, 13-4-41
Frederick Raymond Kerr, Australia, 23-4-41
Christopher Champain Tanner, England, 23-5-41
Norman Atherton Wodehouse, England, 4-7-41
William Alexander Ross, Scotland, 28-9-41
Edward William Francis De Vere Hunt, Ireland, 20-12-41
Vivian Gordon Davies, England, 23-12-41
Cecil Rhys Davies, Wales, 24-12-41
Clifford Walter Patrick Lang, Australia, 4-3-42
Hubert Dainton 'Trilby' Freakes, England, 10-3-42
Patrick Munro, Scotland, 3-5-42
Lewis Alfred Booth, England, 26-6-42
Kenelm Mackenzie (Mac) Ramsay, Australia, 1-7-42
James McPhail Ritchie, Scotland, 6-7-42
John Joseph Clune, Ireland, 12-9-42
John Gordon Scott Forrest, Scotland, 19-9-42
Roy Muir Kinnear, Scotland, 22-9-42
Michael Clifford, Australia, 9-10-42
John Berchmans Minch, Ireland, 8-11-42
Drummond St. Clair Ford, Scotland, 12-12-42
Francis Ebsworth Hutchinson, Australia, 4/5-1-43

Final Scrum

Edwin Sautelle Hayes, Australia, 12-1-43
Anderson Gerrard, England, 22-1-43
Eric Ebsworth Hutchinson, Australia, 27-1-43
John Raymond Evans, Wales, 8-3-43
Henri Levée, France, 26-3-43
Georges Yvan 'Géo' André, France, 4-5-43
Reginald Vere Massey Odbert, Ireland, 18-7-43
Robert Alexander, Ireland, 19-7-43
George Roberts, Scotland, 2-8-43
William Mitchell Penman, Scotland, 3-10-43
Herbert James Michael Sayers, Ireland, 6-12-43
Russell Lindsay Frederick Kelly, Australia, 25-12-43
George Holmes Gallie, Scotland, 16-1-44
Alastair Simpson Bell McNeil, Scotland, 26-1-44
George Fletcher Hart, New Zealand, 03-06-44
William Norman Renwick, Scotland, 15-6-44
Maurice Joseph Lawson Turnbull, Wales, 5-8-44
Winston Philip James Ide, Australia, 12-9-44
Roger Claudel, France, 8-12-44
Allan Henry Muhr, France, 29-12-44
Eric Henry Liddell, Scotland, 21-2-45
Etienne Piquiral, France, 13-3-45
Georges Vaills, France, 30-3-45
Robert Michael Marshall, England, 12-5-45

Appendix Two

Alphabetical order
Alexander, Robert, Irish, 19-7-43
André, Georges Yvan 'Géo', France, 4-5-43
Black, Bryan Henry, England, 29-7-40
Booth, Lewis Alfred, England, 25 / 26-6-42
Claudel, Roger, France, 8-12-44
Clifford, Michael, Australia, 9-10-42
Clune, John Joseph, Ireland, 12-9-42
Cobden, Donald Gordon, New Zealand, 11-8-40
Cooke, Paul, England, 28-5-40
Coote, Patric Bernard, Ireland, 13-4-41
Davies, Cecil Rhys, Welsh, 24-12-41
Davies, Vivian Gordon, England, 23-12-41
Dorward, Thomas, Scotland, 5-3-41
Doussau, Emile, France, 28-4-40
Evans, John Raymond, Wales, 8-3-43
Ford, Drummond St. Clair, Scotland, 12-12-42
Forrest, John Gordon Scott, Scotland, 14-9-42
Freakes, Hubert Dainton, England, 10-3-42
Gallie, George Holmes, Scotland, 16-1-44
Gerrard, Ronald Anderson, England, 22-1-43
Hallaran, Charles Francis George Thomas, Ireland, 21-3-41
Hart, George Fletcher, New Zealand, 03-06-44
Hayes, Edwin Sautelle, Australia, 12-1-43
Hunt, Edward William Francis De Vere, Ireland, 20-12-41
Hutchinson, Eric Ebsworth, Australia, 21-1-43
Hutchinson, Francis Ebsworth, Australia, 4 / 5-1-43
Ide, Winston Philip James, Australia, 12-9-44
Kelly, Russell Lindsay Frederick, Australia, 25-12-43
Kerr, Frederick Raymond, Australia, 23-4-41
Kinnear, Roy Muir, Scotland, 22-9-42
Lang, Clifford Walter Patrick, Australia, 4-3-42
Levée, Henri, France, 26-3-43
Liddell, Eric Henry, Scotland, 21-2-45
Luddington, William George Ernest, England, 10-1-41

Mackenzie, Donald Kenneth Andrew, Scotland, 12-6-40

Marshall, Robert Michael, England, 12-5-45

McNeil, Alastair Simpson Bell, Scotland, 26-1-44

Meret, François, France, 10-6-40

Minch, John Berchmans, Ireland, 8-11-42

Muhr, Henry, France, 29-12-44

Munro, Patrick Munro, Scotland, 3-5-42

Obolensky, Prince Alexander Sergeevich, England, 29-3-40

Odbert, Reginald Vere Massey, Ireland, 18-7-43

Parsons, Ernest Ian, England, 14-8-40

Penman, William Mitchell, Scotland, 3-10-43

Piquiral, Etienne, France, 13-3-45

Ramsay, Kenelm Mackenzie, Australia, 1-7-42

Renwick, William Norman, Scotland, 15-6-44

Rew, Henry, England, 11-12-40

Ritchie, James McPhall, Scotland, 6-7-42

Roberts, George, Scotland, 2-8-43

Ross, William Alexander, Scotland, 28-9-41

Sayers, Herbert James Michael, Ireland, 6-12-43

Tanner, Christopher Champain, England, 23-5-41

Teden, Derek Edmund, England, 15-10-40

Turnbull, Maurice Joseph Lawson, Wales, 5-8-44

Vaills, Georges, France, 30-3-45

Wodehouse, Norman Atherton, England, 4-7-41